RV LIVING
FOR BEGINNERS
Collection (2-IN-1)

The #1 Full-Time RV Living Box Set for Travelers

JEREMY FROST

© Copyright 2019 Jeremy Frost - All rights reserved.

It is not legal to reproduce, duplicate, or transmit any part of this document in either electronic means or in printed format. Recording of this publication is strictly prohibited, and any storage of this document is not allowed unless with written permission from the publisher except for the use of brief quotations in a book review.

ISBN: 978-1-989635-44-5 (Paperback)
ISBN: 978-1-989635-45-2 (Hardcover)

CONTENTS

The Rv Passive Income Guide vii
    Introduction 1
    Chapter One: What Exactly Is Passive Income And How You Can Use It To Your Advantage 7
        Active Income Versus Passive Income: What You Need To Know 8
        The Success Mindset And How To Achieve It 9
        Dispelling The Myths And Lies About Passive Income 13
        Choosing A Business Model: How To Avoid Shiny Object Syndrome 15
        Chapter Summary 17
    Chapter Two: How To Earn A Great Income As A Freelancer 21
        How To Make Your First Dollar Online 22
        What Kind Of Freelancing Can You Do? 24
        What Are The Best Platforms For Freelancers? 25
        How And Why To Reinvest Your Earned Income 30
        Chapter Summary 35
        Chapter Resources 35
    Chapter Three: Mastering The Art Of Self-Publishing For Profit 39
        What Exactly Is Self-Publishing? 39
        Selecting A Niche That Will Make You Money 40
        How To Publish Your Very First Book-What You Need To Include 42
        Should You Write Your Book Yourself or Outsource It? 44
        Creating A Stunning And Eye-Catching Cover 44
        Should You Turn Your Book Into An Audiobook? 46
        How And Why You Should Distribute Your Book On Multiple Platforms 49
        Chapter Summary 52
        Chapter Resources 54

Chapter Four: How To Build A Blogging Business For Sustainable Income 55
What Is Blogging - In A Nutshell 55
Journaling Vs. Authority Vs. Niche Sites, What's The Best? 56
How Bloggers Make Money and How You Can To! 57
Where You Find Your Audience and Get Eyeballs On Your Site 60
What Is SEO And Why It's So Important 63
Chapter Summary 65
Chapter Resources 67

Chapter Five: YouTube Success Secrets Revealed 69
How To Get Started With YouTube 69
Growing Your Subscriber Base 73
Getting Paid-Active And Passive Income Ideas 79
Chapter Summary 84
Chapter Resources 85

Chapter Six: The Secrets To Affiliate Marketing Only The Pros Know 87
What Is Affiliate Marketing? 87
The Best Affiliate Companies to Join 89
How Exactly Do Affiliates Earn Money? 91
Why It's Better To Sell Other People's Products 98
Do You Actually Need A Website To Be An Affiliate? 99
Chapter Summary 100
Chapter Resources 102

Chapter Seven: Essential Amazon FBA Tactics To Grow Your Business 103
What Is Amazon FBA? 103
How To Select Winning Products That Sell! 107
Where Can I Find Products To Source? 109
Cashing In: How To Make Money With Amazon FBA 112
The Essentials Of Running Amazon Ads 113
Chapter Summary 116
Chapter Resources 118

Chapter Eight: Everything You Need To Know About Selling
Your Business For A Big Payout 119
  Why You Should Build A Business With Selling In Mind 120
  When Is The Right Time To Sell Your Business? 123
  How To Work With A Broker To Sell Your Business 125
  Rinse And Repeat For Maximum Profits 127
  What Types Of Businesses Are Brokers Looking For 127
  Chapter Summary 130
  Chapter Resources 132
 Final Words 133
 Resources 135

The Rv Lifestyle Manual 141
 Introduction 145
 Chapter 1: You Have Way Too Much Stuff! 149
  Downsizing for the Count 150
  Evaluating Future Purchases 162
 Chapter 2: Choosing the Right RV for You 165
  Points to Remember Before Buying an RV 165
  Important Myths to Debunk 172
  Types of RVs 174
  Floor Plans to Think About 179
  Learning to Drive Your RV 183
 Chapter 3: Transitioning into the RV Lifestyle 187
  Adjusting to Your New Life on the Road 187
  How to Survive Living in a Small Space! 189
  Traveling With Kids and Animals 193
  Tips for RVing With Pets 198
  Making Your RV Feel like Home 199
 Chapter 4: What You Need to Know Before You Go! 205
  How Do You Dump the Tanks? 205
  Regular Maintenance on the Road 210

v

    Why Your RV Needs to be Level 213

    What to Do If the RV Breaks Down 215

    Electricity and Power 219

Chapter 5: Camping and Boondocking Basics 225

    What is Boondocking All About? 225

    How to Camp for Free All Over the World 226

    RV Clubs and Memberships 231

    Long-Term and Short-Term Parking Options for Your RV 233

Chapter 6: Making Money on the Road 237

    Finding Seasonal Work 238

    Why Freelance Work Might Be Right for You 240

    Working at the Campground 242

    How to Start Earning Passive Income Online 243

Chapter 7: Solo RVing Done Right 251

    Don't Let Being by Yourself Stop You! 251

    Staying Safe on the Road 254

    Avoiding Loneliness 256

    Connecting With the Community 260

Chapter 8: Commonly Asked Questions 263

    What is the worst thing about living in an RV? 263

    What is the best thing about RV life? 264

    How can you do laundry? 265

    Do you feel safe on the road? 266

    Isn't gas mileage terrible? 267

    When will you start living a normal life again? 267

    Can you RV full-time in the winter? 267

    How do you stay in shape while on the road? 268

    Do you get tired of living in a small space? 268

    What do you do with all the poop? 268

Conclusion 269

References 271

THE RV PASSIVE INCOME GUIDE

Learn The Laptop Lifestyle And Swap Your Day Job For Full-Time RV Living

JEREMY FROST

Formal education will make you a living;
self-education will make you a fortune.
— *Jim Rohn*

INTRODUCTION

When was the last time you truly felt free? Free to jump in your RV and go see all of the places that you have always wanted to see?

I'm going to guess that right now you are stuck in the 9-5 grind, desperately wanting to downsize your life, purchase and move into your dream RV, and go experience all of those places on your bucket list that you have only ever seen other people travel to. Or, perhaps, you already own your dream RV but can only travel as far as a weekend will take you.

There is one big problem staring you in the face - your travel options are drastically limited because you have to return to your soul-sucking job every week on Monday. Then you spend the next five days dreaming about taking your next RV trip, only to be left obsessing about having to go back to work on Monday again.

Let's face it - traveling takes money. Even if you have a good chunk of change saved up, you are still going to need to pay bills, like your cell phone and insurance. Your savings can get eaten up really fast if you consistently have money going out and nothing coming back into your savings or checking account.

Even if you are downsizing, you still have to consider expenses like gas, food, insurance, parking, and activities - unless you only ever plan on parking in the WalMart parking lot. You want to quit your job and go on the road traveling in your RV, living the lifestyle that you see all over social media. But in order to quit your job and live your dream life, you need to find a way to make money while you are traveling in your RV.

Or win the lottery, but let's not count on that...

You might have heard stories about how people have made great money online and are now able to travel full time. It seems like every time you scroll through Instagram, you see new posts about someone traveling full time. But is that really something that YOU can do?

Without a doubt...YES!

It is possible to make a very good income online without having to sacrifice the best hours of the day. The best part is that you can even make some really great passive income so you can actually enjoy your time traveling and not be stuck at a computer all day long, because there is no point in living in an RV full-time if you can't actually go anywhere or do anything!

This guide is going to teach you everything a beginner needs to know to get started making money online so you can live your laptop lifestyle, quit your time-consuming day job, and join the ranks of full-time RV living!

In this book, you are going to learn a variety of ways to earn income online that will continue to pay you well into the future. Each chapter reviews a different business model where you will get actionable steps on how to proceed with each business so you will have success from the start rather than trying to reinvent the wheel.

Starting an online business can be scary - especially if you have never done anything like it before - but it doesn't have to be. Once you are armed with the knowledge of how to start an online business, you can tackle your new adventure with confidence and excitement every day.

But why the heck should you listen to some guy you have never met before?

Hi, I'm Jeremy Frost!

Although I have been a full-time RVer for over five years, which I spoke about in my previous book *The RV Lifestyle Manual*, many people don't realize that I started my journey with little savings and just a laptop. My interest in online business started many years before I hit the open road with my RV and although I didn't plan it at the time, these two things created the perfect marriage for me to live out my dream lifestyle.

And you can do it too!

In this book, I'm going to give you all the essentials that took me years of failure and persistence to learn how to be successful.

Your time on this planet is limited, and there is no reason you shouldn't be doing what you love. Stop just settling and living your life to make someone else money.

Go see the world, have new experiences, wake up every day with a sense of purpose and passion. You aren't in this world to just work, pay taxes, and die. This guide is going to give you the tools you need to start living your best life, on your own terms!

But I must warn you...

This isn't one of those get rich quick schemes, pyramid schemes, or multi-level marketing buy-ins, and you won't be trying to push weight loss pills and powders to your friends and family on your social media profiles.

I am talking about creating a real, sustainable business with products and or services that will not only help people but will continue to pay you for years to come while doing something you actually enjoy and are passionate about. Real businesses take time, effort, and planning. What I'm going to show you in this book is that building a real business is a lot less complicated than you might think.

Once your business is generating a real and sustainable income, you will be able to travel, not ever have to worry about waking up to that annoying alarm clock (if you don't want to), or just hang out with your friends, all while your business is making money for you. That is if you are doing this correctly. The power to live the lifestyle you want is in creating systems and processes that generate passive income.

Over the last several years, I have helped fellow full-time RVers make passive income online, and it has dramatically changed their lives for the better. Not to brag, but I can't tell you how many thank you emails and praise I have received from helping other people learn to make passive income online so that they can live their best lives. Heck, I even get the occasional snail mail in my P.O. Box here and there. I love the feeling of helping others achieve their dreams and break out of a life they think they have to live because that is what society tells them they have to do!

I hope to be able to spread this passive income guide throughout the RV community and be able to help thousands of more people each and every year.

While I wish that everyone who reads this book can create a business that earns them six-figures per year, like myself, I can't guarantee how much you will make. It all depends on your ability to take consistent action and implement the things you learn in this book. It's unfortunate, but many of you will read this book, get excited about building a business, but never actually do it!

What I can promise you is if you take action right now, you will earn your first dollar of passive income online within 30 days of finishing this book. It might only be enough for a small coffee, or you might make enough to cover your bills for the next month, it all comes down to how much effort you are willing to put into your business.

Think about it, if you can make your first dollar (or more) in a month from now, what can you do in three months, then six months? How badly do you want to hand in your resignation at work and pack up your RV without having a set date that you need to come back?

This guide is going to show the differences between earned income and passive income while dispelling some of the myths of each. Then we will cover the passive income models that have been proven to work for me, *Jeremy Frost*, and make me six-figures a year consistently.

We all already know that we live in a technology era. Many of the best opportunities to earn substantial passive income are wide open right now. Gone are the days of having to invest huge chunks of money into real estate to be able to generate a passive income. There is lots of money to be made, a low barrier to entry, and much less competition. This is only going to change in the future as things will become more competitive, and people start to embrace the laptop lifestyle and realize that they don't have to work 9-5 anymore.

So you could read this book, think *"oh that's nice for him, he probably had some special advantage, blah blah, blah"* and do nothing.

OR…

You can read this book and take the necessary steps to start building your laptop lifestyle so you can quit your day job and live the full-time RV life.

The time is now! Take action on what you learn in this book and set yourself up for success and financial freedom for the rest of your life. Travel the world in your RV, spend time with your friends and family, and make new memories. I'm going to show you how I've done all of this and more by earning a passive income online, and you can do it too!

So let's get started!

CHAPTER ONE
What Exactly Is Passive Income And How You Can Use It To Your Advantage

You might think that passive income is only for those that are already wealthy - multi-millionaires with portfolios of hundreds of thousands of real estate holdings and such. While many people who are already wealthy have several streams of passive income, it is not some big secret and exclusive thing that only those "in the know" understand how to do.

Did you know that the average millionaire has seven different streams of income?

I'm going to let you in on a little secret "they" don't want you to know about...

ANYONE CAN CREATE PASSIVE INCOME!

There, the cat's out of the bag.

It doesn't matter if you were born into money or are living paycheck to paycheck. With a little bit of knowledge and a lot of hard work, anyone can create a business that generates passive income.

In this chapter, we are going to cover the difference between active and passive income, how you can prime your mindset for success, and why trying to be perfect is the wrong thing to do. I will also dispel some of the myths of passive income and how to avoid shiny object syndrome.

ACTIVE INCOME VERSUS PASSIVE INCOME: WHAT YOU NEED TO KNOW

But what's the difference between passive income and just regular old (otherwise known as active) income?

Active income is when you go to your job, put in your hours, and get paid. You have to be ACTIVELY working to earn the income and it is generally an hourly wage or a salary. You call in sick...you don't get paid. You get fired, then you really don't get paid.

Passive income is income that you earn that "requires little to no daily effort to maintain," (Hogan, 2019). Passive income is not just something where you flip a switch or click a few links and you are generating thousands of dollars per day. If someone promises you this, run far away, it is a scam!

Passive income is actually built by putting in a lot of effort in the beginning to build something that then makes you money even when you are not working on it. Heck, it can even make you money while you sleep! Imagine, when you are generating passive income, log into your bank account and it has increased, without you doing any additional work! It really is an amazing feeling.

There are many benefits to creating a passive income, beyond just being able to travel when and where you want in your RV. Passive income helps to build wealth, gives you the ability to retire early (or start RVing sooner), provides protection in the case that you would lose your primary source of income, and provides you with additional income if you outlive your retirement funds.

The primary benefit of passive income in the RV lifestyle is that you can travel, make money, and not have to worry about working all the time. You get to actually enjoy your life and your travels.

You are not going to become a millionaire overnight with passive income (if it were that easy, everyone would do it!). You can, however, build up some serious streams of income over the long run. Depending on what kind of business (or businesses) you are building, passive income can mean a few thousand dollars a month to hundreds of thousands of dollars...PER MONTH!

Now, I know that might sound crazy at this point, especially if you haven't even made your first dollar online. But believe me, it is completely achievable. Once you start seeing what is really possible, it becomes real and not just a dream anymore.

There are literally tons of ways to create passive income online. The ones that we are going to address in this book are self-publishing, freelancing, blogging, YouTube, affiliate marketing, Amazon FBA, and selling your business for a big payday.

You might also consider if you already own a home and are going to be traveling in your RV full-time, renting out your home for passive income each month. Look at other comparable rental properties in your area, how much do you think you could charge? What is your current mortgage? While this is not a topic that we cover in this book, it is something to take into consideration.

THE SUCCESS MINDSET AND HOW TO ACHIEVE IT

The first step in building your business is getting your mindset right. Your mindset has more to do with your success then you realize.

There is one thing that successful people realize that many others do not - time is their most valuable asset. If you want to truly build wealth, you have to value your time more than you value money. When it comes to making money online many people have this instant gratification mindset. They want to make money yesterday. They aren't willing to plant their tree for the future.

You need to be willing to sacrifice for a while before you start making a steady income.

Your mindset is so important when it comes to building your business. You can have the most amazing website, write the best book, follow all the right marketing strategies, but if your mindset isn't right, then you aren't going to reach your full entrepreneurial potential.

Perhaps you think that you weren't meant to be an entrepreneur. Get that out of your head right now! If you have the passion, the drive, the knowledge, and are willing to work for it, then you ARE meant to be an entrepreneur! There are so many successful entrepreneurs that started their own businesses after being fired from their jobs.

There is a reason you picked up this book, there is a reason you were drawn to earning income online so that you can travel in your RV full time and live your best life. People who are not meant to be entrepreneurs don't read about this kind of stuff. They are happy working their 9-5 jobs and never looking for anything different.

Remember when you were young and your mother told you that you could be anything you wanted to be when you grew up? She wasn't lying. As we get older our mindsets change from playing make-believe that we are explorers and letting our imaginations run wild. The reality of paying bills and working for someone else smacks you in the face and your dreams slowly die. But it doesn't have to be that way! You can be an entrepreneur, you can live your best life, and travel the world on your own terms.

You also have to keep in mind that to fail is part of the process. You learn a lot from your mistakes and from your failures. Your journey into entrepreneurship is not going to be perfect. The process of becoming an entrepreneur and building your business is just as important as the end product of the passive income you will make. Don't worry about doing everything perfect, worry about your progress.

Perfection is the enemy of progress

It is better to get your website up and running, even if you think it's ugly, even if it's not fully optimized. Making something and putting it out into the world is going to get you to your goal faster than if you don't do anything until it's perfect.

With the mindset of not being good enough, you also might think that you are too late to jump on this online income bandwagon. This is simply not true! You actually have a huge advantage to starting later, you learn from other people's mistakes, find loopholes, and scope out your competition. While you might think competition is a bad thing, it's not. Having competition in your market means that there is a need for your business.

Don't fall into the trap of making excuses not to get started. You are never too old and it is never too late. The best time to start your business is now with what you already have! There is no magical "right" time to get started.

Don't go at it alone

Just because you are going to be using the internet to make your income doesn't mean that you should be doing it alone. In fact, you shouldn't be doing it alone at all! While being an entrepreneur can be lonely, you should make it a point to connect with others that are in a similar situation and build relationships.

Perhaps there is someone that you found online that is where you would like to be in a year or two, reach out to them. Generally speaking, entrepreneurs love helping one another. If you don't want to reach out to someone individually, try attending a conference where you can meet people that are doing the same type of thing you are doing. This is a great opportunity to connect with other entrepreneurs and industry leaders.

There are hundreds of conventions held throughout the world every year for business owners and entrepreneurs of all kinds. You can also find local meetups in your area for entrepreneurs. Meet people any way you can, create connections, and build relationships.

There is one core thing to remember with this though, always give before you take. Don't email someone saying how much you admire them and off the bat ask them to mentor you for free; you likely won't get a great response. If you really want to be mentored by someone, then you need to establish a relationship with them first.

Work on your mindset every day. It is like a muscle, you can train it to work for you. Say positive affirmations about your business rather than saying negative things that will steer your mindset in a negative direction.

DISPELLING THE MYTHS AND LIES ABOUT PASSIVE INCOME

Just as with everything else online, there are many myths around passive income. Here we are going to go over some of the most common myths related to passive income.

The set it and forget it method

There is no set it and forget it method that is going to generate you hundreds of dollars a day. While there are a ton of "programs" online that tout they have the answer to 100% passive income where you push a few buttons and you will be generating millions of dollars online without ANY work, these are straight-up scams. They take advantage of people that are unfamiliar with the online business space. Do not EVER sign up for anything that promises these types of claims.

Real income takes real work.

Even things like real estate investing and websites you need to check in on once in a while to make sure they are still working and doing what you want them to do, all still require work. Unfortunately, there is no such thing as 100% hands-off, passive income. You can, however, invest time upfront to get everything up and running then check on things periodically to make sure everything is still generating you the money you want without sucking up all of your time and energy. Or you can hire someone to run it for you.

You can set it up quickly

The goal of passive income is to be able to not only generate you money but also give you time freedom. While it does take a lot of time and energy to get your passive income streams initially set up, once everything is up and running you shouldn't have to put as much time and effort into building the business. Instead, more of your efforts will go into sustaining it. Once the business is built you can find ways to automate things through software and outsourcing as we've already discussed.

Remember

Creating passive income has just as much to do with your mindset, as we discussed before, then it does with your knowledge and hard work. Some people don't believe what you think really matters, but what you think is what becomes your reality. If you think you aren't cut out to be an entrepreneur, then you aren't. If you think that you can create streams of passive income to live your best life traveling in your RV, then that is what is going to happen. Squash those limiting beliefs and get your mindset right before anything else.

You only need one good income source

Remember earlier when I said that on average millionaires have seven different income streams? Well, if they are already millionaires, there is a reason they have multiple income streams. Think about this, if the only way you generate revenue is with your job, what happens when you get fired? No more revenue. The same goes for building a business. Say you publish a book, one book, and it does really well and that is your only revenue stream. Suddenly, something happens, your book gets blacklisted, banned by Amazon and all major retailers. You are out of income!

This is why millionaires generate multiple passive income streams - to stay millionaires.

You need money to make money

There is a really big misconception that you need to invest thousands of dollars in order to get started making money online. The people who are making you believe that are the ones making money from selling thousand-dollar courses on how to make money online.

Do you see the trend there?

You can start a self-hosted blog (more on that in Chapter Four) for less than $100. You can publish a book on Amazon or start freelancing for literally nothing.

While you are going to need a lot more capital if you are planning on investing in real estate, it is possible to start an online business for $0!

CHOOSING A BUSINESS MODEL: HOW TO AVOID SHINY OBJECT SYNDROME

Starting an online business can lead you down one giant rabbit hole. The more you learn about creating a business online, the more you want to learn about it, and there are millions of programs you can buy, coaches you can work with, and businesses that you can try.

But that is not the goal here. The goal is to choose a business model that will work for you and stick with it. Now you can certainly create other businesses in the future, but only after you have one that is successful and that is generating you income.

Back to the whole instant gratification thing…

People are impatient. When they want something, they want it now, and having a successful business is no different. You can't expect to open your virtual doors and have people flooding through with credit cards in hand. It just doesn't work that way. You have to be willing to put in the work and wait to reap the long-term rewards.

Your online business is not *Field of Dreams*, no one is going to come because you built it.

When you decide to open an online business there are going to be challenges, believe me! Success is not a straight line, there are hills, potholes, rivers to cross, and mountains to climb. Don't give up when you come to that river. Instead, fall in, build a bridge, then cross it. There are going to be plenty of times where you think to yourself, *"What am I doing?! Why am I doing this?!,"* but don't give up too soon. There is a famous quote by Thomas Edison, *"I didn't fail, I just found 10,000 ways it didn't work."*

It is very exciting when you first start your business and everything is new. However, over time that excitement will wear off and you might want to say forget it and move onto something else, maybe something that you think is going to be easier or more fun or make you more money. As an entrepreneur, it is very easy to get distracted by shiny objects and never really, fully commit to your business. What many people don't realize is that the newest tactic is not what moves the needle on your business, it is the core fundamentals that keep you moving forward in your business.

If you dabble in your business you are never going to get very far. Whichever path you choose, you should go all in, become a master of your business niche. Invest in yourself and your business in things that will bring you - and your customers - value.

You are going to need to abandon short-term thinking and start to think long-term. It's going to take a lot of work and you might not see the results you want for months or even longer. Get rid of your distractions - instead of sitting down and watching TV at night, work on building your business. You don't need to start from scratch, there are plenty of resources online to help you get started. While there are many great, free resources available, don't be afraid to invest in yourself. Although make sure you do your research before you buy any program or course to make sure that the person selling it isn't just there to take your money and run.

You truly have unlimited potential inside of you, don't waste it!

CHAPTER SUMMARY

Passive income is income that you receive for work that you have previously done. Active income is where you have to be actively working in order to get paid (like a regular 9-5 job).

Anyone can create passive income streams. You don't have to already be rich and hire a team to start generating passive income. Passive income takes work to establish, more so in the beginning and not so much on a daily basis once you have it set up.

There is no such thing as flipping a switch and clicking a few links to generate passive income, these are scams!

There are many benefits to passive income:

- Financial freedom
- Additional protection
- Can create multiple streams
- Time freedom

Before you decide on what type of business you are going to build, you need to get your mind right first. Mindset is everything when it comes to building a business. If you believe you will succeed, then you will. If you have a negative mindset that you are never going to make it, then that is exactly what is going to happen.

Building passive income is like planting a money tree for the future. It's not going to bloom overnight, it's going to take time. The wealthy realize that time is more valuable than money and build their businesses accordingly. Don't let your imagination and your dreams die.

Don't try and be perfect. You are going to make mistakes and you are going to fail. That is part of the process. I have never met another entrepreneur that hasn't failed and made mistakes. The important thing is that you learn from them and don't get discouraged.

Learn from other people's mistakes as well. Having a bit of competition is a good thing, it means that there is a demand to be fulfilled.

Stop waiting for the right time and just start now!

Connect with other entrepreneurs through meetups, conferences, and conventions. Build relationships with others in your space. If you blog, reach out to other bloggers, and so forth.

There is no set and forget method to passive income, period. Don't believe anyone who says otherwise, they are just going to take your money and run.

It is going to take time and effort to actually start to generate passive income. It is also in your best interest to generate multiple streams of passive income so you never have to worry about having to go back to your job because you lost your one stream of passive income. You also don't need a huge monetary investment to get started. Just your time and a lot of work.

Do your best to avoid shiny object syndrome and focus on one main business to start with rather than being all over the place. This will make growing your business a lot easier. Don't give up too soon, keep your head up, even when you feel like you might be failing.

There are going to be challenges and you need to rise above them. Stick to the core fundamentals to keep your business growing.

Tap into your potential and get started!

In the next chapter, we are going to cover all about how you can get started making your first dollar online, even if you have never previously made money online or operated a business in your life.

CHAPTER TWO
How To Earn A Great Income As A Freelancer

Although people don't often view freelancing as your typical passive income work, it is the fastest and most effective way to make your first dollar online. Rather than having to build a whole business from scratch and learn a new skill set, you can use the skills you already have to start building an income. You can then reinvest that income into another business that will allow you more passive opportunities.

Often times, making your first dollar online has nothing to do with your skill set but rather your mindset. If you have never owned a business or made money outside of your normal job, then you have been stuck in an employee mindset. Having an employee mindset is not going to get you to your passive income goals. While freelancing is not going to make you millions in your sleep, it is a great way to get your foot in the door and start to learn about the ins and outs of making money online.

You probably already have some skills that you don't even realize that you can use to become a freelancer. So keep reading to find out how you can start your first online business with nothing but your knowledge, a computer, and a lot of hard work and determination.

There are so many great things about freelancing and living the RV life! For starters, you get to pick your own hours, how much work you take on, and which clients you work with. With freelancing, you can take on as much or as little work as you like. Want to visit a more expensive location? Take on another client project or two to fund your fun!

In this chapter, we are going to cover how to make your first dollar online as a freelancer, what you can freelance, what the best platforms are for freelancers, if freelancing can actually be passive, and how and why you should reinvest your earned income.

HOW TO MAKE YOUR FIRST DOLLAR ONLINE

There are millions of freelancers online doing a wide variety of various jobs and tasks to earn income. Some even earn a rather substantial income from freelancing, but it's not easy. Building your presence and your client base online takes a lot of work and dedication. However, once you have a good client base built up, it can be pretty easy to get repeat business and a reliable income every month.

I would like to first address the differences between a freelance job versus a gig or contract worker. Freelancers can be hired on just like a regular employee or on a contract basis. There are advantages and disadvantages to each.

Freelance employee

Being hired as a freelance worker to a company gives you the freedom to work from anywhere your RV takes you (as long as there is WiFi). Many of the freelance positions available offer time flexibility as well, meaning you don't have to be "clocked in" at certain times. You might, however, have to attend team meetings at certain times. Just make sure you are getting your time zone conversions correct! Being employed as a freelancer can also provide the benefit of health care insurance, paid time off, and other employee type benefits. You also benefit from consistent work, either for clients or for the company itself.

The major disadvantage is that you are still working for someone. You might have to take on clients that you don't want to work for or don't really like. Depending on the position, you might not have too much time flexibility as well. It varies from company to company.

Independent freelancer

Working gigs or being a contract employee can allow you a bit more freedom but also comes with its own set of challenges. If you choose to go out on your own, you are going to need to build your own client base, which can take time. The great thing about this is you get to choose who you work for and what you are charging. You don't have to worry about reporting to anyone other than your clients and can work when and where you want to.

The biggest disadvantage to this is that you don't get any kind of employee benefits. While this can be hard for some people to swallow, especially if you have always been used to having health insurance through an employer, there are options. You can check out the self-employment section of HealthCare.Gov or see if your home state offers some type of state insurance for self-employed people.

Once you have determined which type of freelancing you would like to do and you have an idea of what skills you are going to be using, it's time to start on your search for clients and making that first dollar online.

WHAT KIND OF FREELANCING CAN YOU DO?

There are literally hundreds of different freelancing jobs and gigs available to do online. Here is a list to get you thinking about some of the freelance jobs that you could do:

- Voiceover artist
- Writer/copywriter/ghostwriter/blogger
- Web designer
- Graphic designer
- Virtual assistant
- Social media manager
- Translation
- Transcription
- Illustration
- Video editor
- Songwriter
- Game development
- Mobile app development
- Ecommerce
- Consulting
- Greeting card designer
- Data Entry
- SEO specialist

And that is just a few off the top of my head! While you can certainly learn just about any skill needed for these freelancing positions, there are a few things to keep in mind. You should have an interest in doing this long term and be good at it. You don't want to have just another job, that would kind of defeat the purpose of freelancing to live the RV life. You also want to be sure that you are good at what you do. If you aren't good, it's not likely that you will get repeat customers and referrals for new business.

If your 9-5 is something that you could turn into a freelancing gig that is a great place to start. Perhaps you currently do data entry, or manage your company's social media, use this experience as a starting point. You can always pivot later as your goals change and as you build up a client base.

One of the great things about having a client base is that you can cross-sell or up-sell them on different services. Perhaps you are a freelance writer who has learned how to do social media management. You can cross-sell your services for additional revenue streams.

WHAT ARE THE BEST PLATFORMS FOR FREELANCERS?

There are tons of different freelance platforms online that you can start on. Some of them have a very low barrier to entry, while others take some time to build up a reputation and client base before you can start to get work that actually pays well.

Upwork

Upwork is, in my opinion, one of the best and biggest platforms for freelancers out there. You can find freelance work in everything from web design to customer service. Not only are there many types of freelance work available on Upwork, they make signing up and managing your gigs super easy. As with many other platforms, the more you work on Upwork, the better reviews you get, and the more easily you can find work there. Make sure that you are creating a freelancer profile that really showcases your skills and talents while creating stellar proposals to send to clients. Upwork even offers an app that makes connecting with clients super simple and easy to keep everything organized. Furthermore, the more work you can get through Upwork, the less you will have to pay in fees, so that's a win-win!

Facebook

If you are just starting, look to Facebook. There are thousands of Facebook groups for every kind of freelancing work, as well as general groups. It might take a bit to find one that you like, and that has legit opportunities, but it can be a great place to start. Many of the people in the groups are looking for help within their own businesses and want to help other business owners (that's you, the freelance business owner).

Simply start your Facebook search by typing in relevant keywords in the search bar, such as "writer," "freelance," or "web design," and see what comes up for groups. Join as many groups as you can to get started with, then work your way through the groups to see which ones are going to be the most beneficial to you.

Fiverr

Fiverr is another great place for freelancers to get started. There is a very low barrier to entry, and if you know what you are doing and can create some recurring clients, you can earn a good income. The basic concept of Fiverr was born on creating a service-based business where entrepreneurs and businesses could get help on things like writing blog posts and getting a logo designed for as little as $5.

But fear not, you don't have to worry about just working gigs for $5 each, you can make a lot more on Fiverr! People can make up to $10,000 per transaction on Fiverr (based on their services and experience, of course!).

Working with clients

There are a few things to keep in mind when you start looking for work on freelance platforms. You have to be good and actually know what you are doing! On many freelancer platforms, you get new clients based on your previous reviews. If you have a bad review, you aren't likely to get new clients.

While many communications happen over messaging and email, you might have to TALK to a potential client in order to sell them. When this happens, you have to be sure that you can sell your services when talking to someone. You aren't going to get clients if you don't have a clear message that you are communicating to them and letting them know what you can offer them.

You also need to know your minimum rate and not have to worry about competing against someone who is only charging $5 for their services. There are many different ways to calculate your rate, but make sure to factor in the fees that the freelance platform takes out.

While you might think that it is difficult to compete against someone overseas who is charging only a fraction of what you charge, there is one very large factor that business owners are willing to pay for, and that is quality. A higher-quality product can be produced when both parties fully understand each other. It is not to say that business owners should discount working with someone overseas, but there are many people that prefer to work with someone who is in their region.

You should also be aware of your competitors' prices and why you can charge more. If you are based in the US, you will tend to have an advantage for business owners that are looking to outsource to US freelancers. Once you have some great reviews under your belt, you can certainly start to raise your rates. But don't forget to be realistic here, you can't completely rely on freelance platforms for your income. You are going to need to build up a client base outside of the platforms just like with any other online position. As the old saying goes, you can't put all of your eggs in one basket. You need to diversify and make sure that you are moving towards being able to be in full control of your clients and your income. At any point anything that is a platform can delete all of your information and all the information you have on your clients, then you are left with nothing.

Other freelancer platforms include:

- UpWork (already discussed above)
- Fiverr
- Freelancer
- Envato Studio
- PeoplePerHour-Great for those located in the UK
- TopTal-Great if you are already an expert in your field

You can also look for freelance and remote positions on job board sites as well. Many remote jobs offered on job boards offer plenty of location independence, and you can also find contract and freelance positions rather than traditional "jobs." Freelance writing is very popular to start out with, and there is certainly no shortage of work available.

Some great job boards to start on are:
- Problogger
- ZipRecruiter
- Indeed
- Glassdoor
- LinkedIn
- SmashingJobs
- BloggingPro
- MediaBistro
- SoloGig
- JournalismJobs
- WeWorkRemotely
- Online Writing Jobs
- Freelance Writing
- All Freelance Writing

Use search terms like "remote," "virtual," or "work from home" to search for location-independent positions.

Can freelancing be passive?

This can be a difficult question to answer. While the goal of living the RV lifestyle is to create passive income so that you can spend your time driving to and enjoying destinations that you have always dreamed of, you still have to be able to make money to fund your new lifestyle. But let's face it, if you are spending 8-10 hours a day working (or looking for new work) that doesn't leave you much time to enjoy your new RV lifestyle.

So, no freelancing can not be passive - at least in the beginning. The catch 22 here is that you need to build up a client list of steady income, then you can start to outsource some tasks to other freelancers or a virtual assistant. You can easily offload simple tasks to a VA or other freelancers. For example, if you are a writer, you can hire an editor to edit your work and save you some time having to self-edit.

When you start to hire other people, this is where freelancing can turn into an agency.

For example, if you are a social media manager, once you have built up a good base of clients, you can start hiring other freelancers, that you pay a little less while you act as the project manager or agency manager. So in that type of freelancing, you can generate passive income. However, at this point, it isn't really freelancing as much as building a different business.

There are other ways in which you can create passive income as a freelancer. For example, if you are a social media manager, you can set up accounts for your clients and then invest in some automation software to free up some of your time. If there is any way that you can set up automation systems for what you are currently doing, then you certainly can create passive income streams from your freelancing.

HOW AND WHY TO REINVEST YOUR EARNED INCOME

As with building any business, you should be reinvesting some of your earned income. Any good business owner knows this. But just sticking money back into your business willy nilly isn't going to get you anywhere. You need to know how, why, and what you should be reinvesting in.

I mentioned outsourcing certain tasks in the previous section, but I want to address it here a little differently. Outsourcing can be great for many reasons, mostly because it will give you more time to either do the leisure things you want to do or to work on other areas of your business. Outsourcing some of your tasks allows you to work ON your business rather than IN your business.

Outsourcing

There are also some disadvantages to outsourcing. First of all, it costs money, sometimes a lot, sometimes a little. If you have never managed anyone before, it can be quite an experience. Some people need very little direction to get their work done while others need to be micromanaged. You don't want to hire someone who needs micromanaging. Furthermore, if you outsource to someone who isn't very good, then you have to worry about letting them go and so on. One particular challenge of living the RV life and outsourcing your work is that it can be rather difficult to connect with your team, whether there are drastic differences in time zones or poor WiFi connection.

If you are planning to outsource to someone overseas to try and save some money, do your research! Platforms like onlinejobs.ph offer coaching services for your "employees" for a monthly cost. This is a great option if you have never built a team before and you don't know the first thing about how to manage someone. You can find virtual assistants on onlinejobs.ph in just about every specialty, from Amazon listing specialists to digital content creators. The great thing about hiring someone overseas is that their cost of living is lower. So if you are just starting out hiring a virtual assistant, this can be a great place to start without having to reinvest too much.

Automation

Another area to reinvest your earned income is into automation services. While it depends on your business model, there are a ton of different automation services out there that can help you to complete a variety of tasks.

Take social media management, for example. While you could spend about an hour or so a day scheduling things to Pinterest (per client!), that isn't the best use of your time. If you invested in a Pinterest scheduler - Tailwind is currently the most popular - then you can spend about an hour scheduling out one client's social media for the next month. You just saved yourself about 20-30 hours over the next month! Keep in mind that in this particular example, the client would pay the monthly subscription for Tailwind, not you. Plus, there are plenty of other kinds of automation software out there to help you to automate your business process.

As a freelancer, you can automate a number of your processes. With your email, for example, you can have emails automatically go into certain folders and check them in bulk at certain times rather than sifting through a bunch of unrelated emails. You can also set up processes to have clients automatically book calls with you rather than having to email back and forth to find a time to connect.

You can also automate part of your client onboarding process. This can be done with automated emails and project management tools. However, you want to be very careful with this part; you don't want to pull yourself out of the equation too much. While your client may have hired you to get them results, they are sure to still want to be in contact with you during your working relationship.

While automation is great for saving you time, there are also things that you can do to streamline your processes. For example, you can use a time tracking software that connects to your bookkeeping software to make sending invoices easier. This way you won't have to go through a huge spreadsheet of working times or guess how much time you spent on a project and how much you should invoice someone.

Professional development

You can also reinvest your earned income into continuing your education. This is a big one, freelancers that stay on top of their game are always working to improve themselves. There are so many online courses out there to help you advance your skills. If you are buying a course from an individual just make sure that you do your research, make sure they actually have experience doing what they say they do. You don't want to take a course on copywriting from someone who hasn't or doesn't actually make a living as a copywriter.

If you are unsure of where to start reinvesting your income when it comes to courses and education, Udemy is a great place to start. Udemy offers courses on just about any subject you can think of, from copywriting to Javascript. Their courses are led by reputable and expert instructors and are very affordable. They often run sales where you can get a course for as little as $12.

If you are looking for anything related to online marketing, such as content creation, copywriting, or SEO, then DigitalMarketer.com offers a huge array of both free and paid resources to expand your learning.

When you continually improve your skills, you can offer more value to your clients. When you offer more value, you can charge a lot more without having to work more. Take writing a sales copy letter, for example. When you can show clients results from previous experience and prove that your work will increase their ROI, you can increase your prices without having to worry about losing business.

Online presence

How you present yourself online can make or break your career as a freelancer. If you have a very ugly website (because you are a writer and not a web designer), then that can reflect poorly on you and the quality of work that you do. Now it is not to say that you won't get any work if you have an ugly website, but it can certainly negatively impact your business. Investing in having a strong online presence can help you to land better and higher-paying clients. This could mean investing in a web designer, a social media manager, or a coach to help you take your freelancing business to the next level.

Marketing

Marketing is something that you should never skimp on when it comes to building a business. In order to land clients, they have to know that you exist! Every business should have a marketing budget, whether it's large or small, some of your earned income should be going back into marketing to find new clients. This can be done with things like Facebook Ads, promoted pins to blog posts, or even for attending a conference.

The great thing about being able to invest your earned income back into your freelance business is that living the RV lifestyle allows you less monthly, personal bills that you have to worry about paying. This can leave you with a good chunk of change at the end of each month to reinvest back into your business, which means that you can also grow it quicker.

CHAPTER SUMMARY

Freelancing is a great way to get started making an income online. You can take skills that you already have and turn them into a freelance career. You can either be hired by a company to freelance or work with clients individually; it is ultimately up to you based on your goals.

You can find freelance work through freelance platforms and job boards.

While there is not much passive income when you start out freelancing, there are certain things you can do to work less and make more, such as via outsourcing and automating to increase your passive income.

In order to continue to grow your business, there are certain areas that you should reinvest your earned income back into, such as hiring someone to outsource work to and investing in automation systems and personal development.

CHAPTER RESOURCES

Healthcare for independent freelancers

- HealthCare.Gov

Types of freelance work

- Voiceover artist
- Writer/copywriter/ghostwriter/blogger
- Web design
- Graphic design
- Virtual assistant
- Social media manager

- Translation
- Transcription
- Illustration
- Data Entry
- SEO specialist
- Video editor
- Songwriter
- Game development
- Mobile app development
- Ecommerce
- Consulting
- Greeting card designer

Outsourcing

- Onlinejobs.ph

Professional development

- Udemy
- DigitalMarketer.com

Freelance platforms

- Facebook
- UpWork
- Fiverr
- Freelancer
- Envato Studio
- PeoplePerHour-Great for those located in the UK
- TopTal-Great if you are already an expert in your field

Job boards for freelancers

- Problogger
- ZipRecruiter
- Indeed
- Glassdoor
- LinkedIn
- SmashingJobs-great for developers
- BloggingPro
- MediaBistro
- SoloGig
- JournalismJobs
- WeWorkRemotly
- Online Writing Jobs
- Freelance Writing
- All Freelance Writing

In the next chapter, we will cover exactly how you can make passive income by self-publishing books.

CHAPTER THREE
Mastering The Art Of Self-Publishing For Profit

HAVE YOU EVER dreamed of being a writer? Sitting on the beach with your toes in the sand while you pen your newest manuscript?

The days of having to go through publishing houses and dealing with publishing agents is over. Once your manuscript is complete, you can self-publish it on online platforms and start making money in as little as 24 hours.

In this chapter, we are going to cover what exactly self-publishing is, how you can select a profitable niche, how and where to publish your first eBook, whether you should write the book yourself or outsource it, why you need a cover that grabs your potential reader by the eyeballs, when you should definitely turn your ebook into an audiobook (and when you shouldn't), and finally, whether you should stick to one publishing platform or spread your book out everywhere.

WHAT EXACTLY IS SELF-PUBLISHING?

Self-publishing is just that, a book that you publish yourself.

You write the book then publish it on free platforms like Amazon without ever having it have to be accepted by a publisher or waiting years for a royalty check. The great thing about self-publishing is that you have full control over your book and you get to keep a lot more of the royalties from sales rather than having to share with a publishing house.

When you publish a book through a publishing house there are many restrictions that are placed on the publication. For example, if you wanted to give away a chapter of your book to help get people interested, you can't do that if you are working with a publisher unless they approve. If you are self-publishing your book you can give away a chapter, or heck, even a few free copies to get the word out and have people leave you reviews.

So now that you know what self-publishing actually is, how do you go about knowing what you should write about that people will actually want to pay for to read?

SELECTING A NICHE THAT WILL MAKE YOU MONEY

It's likely that you have a ton of different ideas for book topics. But you don't just want to write about any old topic. You want to write about something that is going to sell and that people actually want to read!

If you haven't already written your book, you are going to want to validate your idea first, before you ever even write your first word. You can do this simply by searching your competition on Amazon.

Search the various categories on Amazon for Kindle best sellers in the eBook category. Within that category you will find many sub-categories such as happiness, motivational, and personal development.

Pick a topic that you want to write about or have started writing about and check out what the top sellers are.

When it comes to sizing up the competition, you want to take a look at that book's Amazon Best Sellers Ranking. You want all the books on the first page of results to have an average BSR of 100,000 or less. Anything above 100,000 shows that the demand for that subject isn't optimal and there are fewer people buying books on that subject.

The second thing you want to look at is how many reviews the books on the first page have, if it's all big authoritative names with hundreds or thousands of reviews you might not be able to compete. However, this is not a hard and fast rule, you have to consider the niche you are writing about. While it might be difficult to get to the #1 best seller for personal development and beat out some very high profile authors, you can certainly size up and beat the competition in a niche like opening a dog boarding business.

The best seller ranking is assigned to a book based on how much it sells. It really all comes down to keywords. The more targeted the book is to an audience, the more likely that the audience is going to purchase that book to solve their problem, and, therefore, the more your book is going to sell.

There are a few other things that you should consider when writing your book. Make sure that you are writing about something that you're passionate about. You don't want to spend months or weeks writing about something you have no interest in. You should also make sure that you are knowledgeable about the topic (it's ok if you aren't, we'll get to that in a minute). It is great if you are writing a book to share your knowledge with the world, but in reality, if you want to write a book on a topic that you don't know much about but you think will sell well, you can always outsource the actual writing.

Now that you have a firm grasp on what your book is going to be about, or perhaps you already have written it, it's time to move onto publishing!

HOW TO PUBLISH YOUR VERY FIRST BOOK-WHAT YOU NEED TO INCLUDE

The hard part is over, you have written your book and are ready to publish it. Self-publishing a book isn't nearly as scary as it sounds. If you are starting on Amazon, which is suggested, the process of uploading your book is very simple.

You want to be sure that your topic is something that people want to read about. Remember, a little bit of competition is a good thing, that means people are buying similar products. Your title and subtitle should grab the reader's attention and address their pain points. When someone reads your title they should want to click the buy now button right away!

An attention grabbing cover

You should also ensure that your book has a cover that is going to grab your reader's attention. The cover should have a clear message and not be too cluttered as to confuse people. Cover design is something that many people outsource, because unless you are already a graphic designer, you aren't going to get the best quality by doing it yourself.

Formatting

You also need to ensure that your book looks great on the inside. Formatting is key here. You don't want huge blocks of text that aren't broken up. Instead, break text into sections, use Bulleted or numbered lists, and images to make the inside of the book more visually appealing. The book should be easy to read as well as easy to scan. Amazon actually offers a mock up type generator that allows you to see what the inside of your look will look like once it has been published on their platform.

Book description

The description of your book is also very important. It is really less of a description and more of a sales letter (Awosika, 2019). This is where you need to focus on your audiences' pain points and how they will be solved when they read your book. The description should really focus on the benefits that the book will provide to the reader.

Using freelancers

Fiverr and Upwork are great platforms to hire freelancers to help you with your book. You can hire freelancers to help you write or ghostwrite the actual book, and book cover designers to help you with developing and creating the most eye-catching cover for your book's niche. You can also hire freelance editors, formatters, and even marketers. Hiring a freelancer is a wonderful option, not only are you helping other entrepreneurs build their business, but you can also find some amazing freelancers for affordable prices.

SHOULD YOU WRITE YOUR BOOK YOURSELF OR OUTSOURCE IT?

There is a dirty little secret in the world of online self-publishing, not all authors write their own books!

I'm just letting all the secrets out!

That's ok though. You see, books can take a very long time to write and if you are a business owner that is running another business, or several other businesses, you might not have time to sit down and write a book. Or perhaps you really want to write a book about a specific topic, such as finances or a fiction romance novel, but you don't have enough knowledge to write an entire book. Or maybe, you just aren't a very good writer.

This is where outsourcing your work will come in handy.

There are plenty of great writers out there that freelance their writing services. They do all the heavy lifting of writing the book, in collaboration with the author of course, then publish it under the author's name. This is called ghostwriting.

There are just as many authors out there who write their own books. If you love writing and you have a strong message or story that you want to tell your audience, then you can probably handle writing your own book.

CREATING A STUNNING AND EYE-CATCHING COVER

People really do judge a book by its cover. While it is good to have some ideas in mind about what you want your cover to look like, you should not even worry about cover design until you have a solid title and subtitle down.

You are going to want to be sure that the cover of your book is sending a clear message and sticking to the norms of the genre's style. Check out the other books in the same genre and take note of what their covers look like. Find your inspiration from other Amazon Kindle best sellers. Perhaps there are certain colors that really stick out to you and catch your eye or types of font you find appealing.

You can also look to social media, specifically Pinterest, for book cover inspiration. Search by genre, topic, color, and niche to find different ideas. Why not try making your own Pinterest board and save all of your great inspiration for when it comes time to design the cover?

While some book covers can be easy to design if you have some skills, you might need to outsource if you are looking for something a little more complicated. If you are looking to design the cover yourself, there are plenty of free templates and tutorials available online. Some great resources for designing the book cover yourself are Canva, Microsoft Word, or Adobe Photoshop and InDesign. If you don't have much experience in design, Canva is a great, user-friendly software to start with.

If you want to leave the cover design to a design professional, there are also many platforms that offer eBook cover design services. Reedsy is a great platform where you can get not only an eBook cover, but also interior design as well by industry leading designers for an affordable price. EBook Launch is another great platform in which you can get eBook covers of all kinds, for fiction, illustrated, and non-fiction.

When you are designing your cover or having a designer do it for you, just make sure you are getting the dimensions of the cover correct. Generally speaking for an Amazon cover it is 2,560 x 1,600 pixels; however, it can change depending on which publication platform you are using. So ensure that you double check the size ratio before designing or having your cover designed.

SHOULD YOU TURN YOUR BOOK INTO AN AUDIOBOOK?

The use of audiobooks has grown exponentially over the past couple of years. While people love to sit down with a good book, they don't always have the time. Purchasing an audiobook allows them to consume the book faster and while they are doing other activities, such as chores, commuting, or working out.

On average, individuals who listen to audiobooks listen to about 15 a year. While the barrier to entry is fairly low for a written book to self-publish on just about any platform, there is a little more involved if you are looking to publish an audiobook as well.

ACX.com is the number one platform when it comes to publishing your audiobook. ACX is a part of Audible and helps to bring together creators, narrators, recording engineers, and even publishers to make you more money with your audiobook. With ACX, your audiobook can be published on Audible, Amazon.com, and iTunes in order to maximize your profits across all platforms. You can audition narrators to find the perfect voice for your book. ACX makes the whole process seamless from making your account to collecting your royalties.

The biggest thing with audiobooks is that you need really high quality sound. While it takes more time and effort to publish an audiobook, in addition to the eBook, the potential profits can be huge, considering the continued growth of the audiobook market.

Now you might think that creating an audiobook isn't for your audience, or that YOU could never narrate your book. First of all, everyone listens to audiobooks!

From the CEO on his/her commute to the office to the stay at home mom driving her kids to band practice, many people from many walks of life listen to audiobooks. The simple fact is if you don't create an audiobook as a companion to your written eBook, you are leaving money on the table that could be going into your pocket (Chesson, 2019a)!

A word of caution though, there are simply some books that do not make good audiobooks. Things like reference or quote books, anything that is very image heavy, such as interior design books, cookbooks, and travel guides. So if your book is one of these, then don't worry about creating an audiobook, it is not going to serve your audience. However, if you are writing romance, health and fitness, business, self-help, history, mystery, or anything related to any of these topics (Chesson, 2019a), then an audiobook is a fantastic idea!

Audiobooks come in many different formats and files, so be sure you are really looking into what type of file is needed before you dive into the creation process. Generally, audiobooks are MP3, M4B, or WAV files. You are also going to have to create another cover for your audiobook, 2400 by 2400 pixels. If you have no idea what that means, don't worry, you can get a cover made on Fiverr for $5.

While recording the audiobook yourself is a very economical option, you can also hire a voice over artist and sound engineer to do the mastering for you.

If you are choosing to record your own audiobook you must ensure that you have quality equipment, which can be an investment in itself if you don't already have it. Things like microphones, headphones, audio interfacing devices, sound eliminators, acoustic equipment, and adequate file storage, and recording/editing software can all add up to hundreds of dollars. If you are planning on doing the narration yourself for multiple books, it might be a worthwhile investment.

However, if you are just starting out and don't want to worry about purchasing a bunch of new equipment, then hiring a voice over artist would be beneficial. The cost of hiring a voice over artist can vary widely depending on many factors; however, it is wise to budget $50 to $200 per finished hour of narration. The price can vary greatly depending on the experience and the quality of the narration. With the ACX.com platform you can find high quality narration talent for $50, which is very affordable and well worth the cost.

Even if you do record everything yourself, send off your recording to an audio engineer. For a rather small cost this can really give your audiobook the pizzaz that it needs upon completion. Also ensure that you are creating a cover specifically for your audiobook. It can be the same design, but adjust the design to match the dimensions for the audiobook distributor.

I have talked a lot about eBooks and audiobooks, but there is one format of book that we haven't covered yet. The paperback or hardcover book. While many people prefer eBooks and listening to audiobooks, you can never discount the classic paperback and hardcover. The smell of a freshly printed book, that crack of the spine the first time you open it, there is nothing else like it. I'm sure I am not the only person to feel this way, so why not cater to your physical book lovers as well?

The great thing about already having an eBook is that you can easily have a physical book printed. And no, I am not talking about ordering 10,000 copies and paying for them in advance just to have them sit in a storage unit somewhere. KDP has the ability to print physical books on demand. One of the best things about print on demand paperback and hardcover books is that you don't have to worry about having a bunch of copies printed right away, but rather you can have them printed as the customer orders them. This can save you a ton of money and frustration.

HOW AND WHY YOU SHOULD DISTRIBUTE YOUR BOOK ON MULTIPLE PLATFORMS

When it comes to the distribution of your book, you have several options. You can choose to publish on Kindle Unlimited or Kindle Select, but this then prohibits you from publishing your book on any other platforms. Or you can publish it as a regular Kindle book and then publish to other platforms like Kobo, Barnes & Noble, or iTunes.

There are several benefits to enrolling into Kindle Unlimited.

- You can put your book on sale for a limited time to create urgency to drive sales.
- You can offer your book for free for a limited time.
- As opposed to getting paid per book you get a cut of the Kindle Unlimited "pool."
- Being part of the Kindle Unlimited and Kindle Owners Lending Library can help to increase your Amazon search rankings (Chesson, 2017).

There are also advantages to publishing your eBook on multiple platforms as well. While Amazon has a GIANT reach, it can also be good to spread things out on different platforms as well. Even if you do only get a small percentage of your sales from other publishing platforms that aren't Amazon, that small percentage can really add up over time.

With Kindle, there are audiences that just don't use the Kindle platform to consume their books and can't use it for one reason or another. Having your book available on other platforms allows for a wider audience in some cases. A platform like Kobo actually has an in-house marketing team to help you get everything up and running.

Using ads to drive traffic to your book

With either Amazon or various other platforms, you can also consider using ads to drive sales to your books rather than just marketing on the platform itself. The biggest thing you have to remember is that no matter which platform you choose, your sales are not guaranteed. You have to be able to actively market your book to your audience in order to get sales. You can't just hit publish and cross your fingers, that is not going to get you very many sales.

While learning about running ads for selling your product (in this case your book) can be a little overwhelming when you are first starting out, there are a few basics to consider. There are two kinds of ads that you can run: automatic and manual. If you are serious about running ads you might want to look into hiring someone to do so as you can quickly lose a lot of money on ads if you don't know what you are doing.

Automatic ads are just that, plug and play - put in a budget, and let your ads run. This can be a great first option if you aren't very familiar with running ads. Just make sure not to set your budget too high. Manual ads require bidding on keywords and keeping a close eye on how your ads are performing. Once you get the hang of it, manual ads aren't as scary as they sound and can greatly help you to drive sales to your book. Running ads are all about keywords - you need to know the keywords you are targeting to generate any kind of traction with your ads.

The platform you choose to publish your book on can vary widely by your audience as well too. It will likely take some time and some experimentation before you figure out what works for you and what resonates with your audience. There are no rules against writing several books and publishing them on various platforms to see what works better for you and your audience. Test, test, and test some more to find out what works, then do more of what works.

Here is a list just to get you started on various platforms that you can publish your book on:

- Amazon Kindle
- Kobo
- Barnes and Noble
- iBook/iTunes
- CreateSpace
- LuLu
- Blurb
- BookBaby
- Bookrix
- Scribd
- Outskirts Press

Just to name a few...

While it can be a lot of work to self-publish a book, especially if you are going to spread your book out through various different platforms, there are tools to make it a lot easier. Platforms like Draft2Digital, Smashwords, and PublishDrive assist in the distribution of your book, help to collect and analyze the book's analytics, collect royalties for you, and pay you out in one transaction rather than having to collect from multiple platforms.

Once your book really starts to take off and you are getting loads of PR, then you can travel to each of your book signings while living your RV life! Not sure how to get PR? You can hire someone for that too!

CHAPTER SUMMARY

You can easily publish a book and start making money is as little as 24 hours. When you self-publish you have full control over the creative process and distribution of your book.

Certain niches are much more profitable than others. Search the Amazon Kindle best sellers list to see what kinds of topics get purchased the most. Shoot for topics that are somewhere between 1,000 and 30,000 on the Kindle best sellers list. But also make sure that you are choosing a topic that you are passionate about.

You can be an author without having to be a great writer. There are many writers that outsource the writing process. Once the book is written it is time to hit publish! Amazon makes it very easy to publish your book with only a few clicks.

Make people want to buy your book with an eye catching cover design, a great title, and attention grabbing sub-title. Put your book into Amazon's mockup generator to ensure that the inside of your book is just as appealing. Your book description should be able to speak to your audience's pain points and address how reading your book can help them.

You can become a self-published author even if you aren't great at writing and don't have the time to write a book. You can outsource the writing to a ghostwriter and still retain the rights to everything.

Take inspiration for your book cover from other book covers in the same genre. You can either design a cover yourself or you can outsource this as well.

Audiobooks are becoming more popular but are more work to get published. Audiobooks are easier to consume and you can generate more profit from them. You can record the audiobook if you already have high quality sound equipment, or you can outsource to a voice over artist.

There are benefits and downfalls to publishing your book on Amazon or on multiple platforms. Ultimately, you need to decide what is best for you and your audience. You can also increase sales by running ads to your book. You need to be sure that you are actively marketing your book, not just hitting publish and waiting for a check to roll in.

If you want to focus on PR, you can hire someone to handle that for you also.

CHAPTER RESOURCES

eBook Cover design

- Canva
- Adobe Photoshop and InDesign
- Reedsy
- EBook Launch
- Fiverr
- Upwork

eBook/audiobook Distribution

- Draft2Digital
- Smashwords
- PublishDrive

Self-Publishing Platforms

- Amazon Kindle
- Kobo
- Barnes and Noble
- iBook/iTunes
- CreateSpace
- LuLu
- Blurb
- BookBaby
- Bookrix
- Scribd
- Outskirts Press
- ACX.com

The next chapter is all about how to earn a great income as a blogger.

CHAPTER FOUR
How To Build A Blogging Business For Sustainable Income

Blogging, just like many other businesses, is what you make of it. The time and effort you put into it, especially in the beginning, will determine how successful you are and ultimately how much money you can make from it. There are well-known bloggers that are making six-figures per month while traveling full time in their RVs.

In this chapter, we are going to cover what exactly blogging is, what the differences are between a journaling site, an authority site, and a niche site. I will also discuss exactly how bloggers make money and how you can apply those concepts to make money with your own blog and how to get people to actually read your blog. Finally, I'll also review what SEO is and why it's so important to your blog.

WHAT IS BLOGGING - IN A NUTSHELL

Way back when the internet was just a baby, people would start online journals, otherwise known as weblogs. As Skrba explains, "A blog (shortening of "weblog") is an online journal or informational website displaying information in reverse chronological order, with the latest posts appearing first. It is a platform where a writer or even a group of writers share their views on an individual subject."

There are many, many websites that either started as a blog or have a blog that is used to promote content to help drive leads to their business. There are two main reasons why someone starts a blog, either for personal reasons or to increase their business' visibility. As a business, if you also have a blog this provides you with more opportunities to gain customers and stay competitive.

JOURNALING VS. AUTHORITY VS. NICHE SITES, WHAT'S THE BEST?

While there are two main reasons to start a blog, there are three distinct types of blogs - journaling, authority, and niche blogs.

Journaling blogs are often started as a personal blog and either stay that way or end up developing into a business driven blog. This can happen after the blogger realizes that their online journaling has struck a chord with a certain audience, and they can actually make money while doing what they love.

Then there are authority sites, such as BuzzFeed, Huffington Post, and The Wirecutter. They can focus on one type of content, in the case of a site like Forbes, or they can focus on a variety of content. The truth is when it comes to authority sites, there isn't much to compete with.

Niche sites, on the other hand, focus on a very specific niche or topic. For example, rather than a site/blog that has only a few popular articles on the RV lifestyle, a niche site would be dedicated to that specific topic. Everything they promote and write about would focus on living the RV lifestyle.

HOW BLOGGERS MAKE MONEY AND HOW YOU CAN TO!

It seems like every day there are more ways that bloggers can earn a great income. As I stated before, there are bloggers out there that are making six-figures per month! While this might not be the most common outcome for many bloggers, there are still a vast number who make a really good income that allows them the freedom to travel full time, whether in an RV or not. There are a few main ways that bloggers can earn money:

- Ads
- Sponsorships
- Digital products
- Affiliate sales
- Services

When you start a self-hosted blog you have the ability to place ads on your site. Self-hosting a blog just means that you are paying a company to host your blog and all of its information. This also means that your domain is something like: mygreatsite.com rather than mygreatsite.wordpress.com. This not only looks much more professional, it's easier to say, and you have WAY more control over what you do with your blog.

By far, Wordpress is the best platform for blogging. It is incredibly easy to use and over a quarter of the internet is run on Wordpress sites. There are two different types of Wordpress sites: Wordpress.com and Wordpress.org. Wordpress.com sites have a domain with something like mygreatsite.wordpress.com, whereas with Wordpress.org you purchase a domain and install Wordpress on your site. So your domain would be something like mygreatsite.com. I talked a little bit about this earlier but it is worth mentioning again.

There are lots of different blogging platforms but using Wordpress is going to give you the most flexibility with your site. Wordpress users have access to thousands of different plugins to allow you to do just about anything you could ever want to do to and with your site, from adding a storefront to creating quizzes. Wordpress is trusted by some of the biggest bloggers out there and also offers great customer service if you ever run into any issues.

Ads

Ad companies pay you, the blogger, to have ads on your site. There are many different ad networks available. One of the most popular for bloggers that are just starting out is Google Adsense. While they don't pay a whole lot, it is a way to get your foot in the door. The great thing about ad income is that it is passive. Once you have the ads set up on your blog, you will continue to get a payout as long as you are getting enough traffic to your blog.

Sponsorships

The next type of income is sponsorships. This is a great way to generate a good and consistent income for your blog. While it can take a little time to start getting opportunities, once you have a few that you can work with on a consistent basis, you can generate a reliable income. Sponsorships can either be one off sponsored posts or a continued working relationship with another company to promote their products and or services to your audience. This can take place through writing blog posts, posting about the company on your social media, sending out information in your email newsletter, or even making a short video.

Digital products

Digital products are another great way to create a passive income stream for your blog. Once you create them you can keep making money from them without much upkeep. Digital products can be anything from ebooks, courses, guides, printables, just about anything that you can create in a digital format that your audience will buy and you don't have to continually work on. You can sell your digital products directly through your blog or use a digital product platform, such as Shopify, Etsy or Clickbank. You can also choose to do both and market your digital products on various platforms. Generally speaking, the more places you are in, the more income you can generate.

Affiliate sales

Affiliate sales can also be another great way to generate some passive income. Here is a great example of how you can create multiple passive income streams from affiliate sales. Say you write a blog post promoting a particular product which pays a pretty good commission, either a one time or recurring commission. You build up a good audience or by chance your post goes viral. Many people are reading your post and decide to purchase the product based on your review or recommendation. You only wrote the post once but you keep earning a commission from it. While you might have to work on marketing the post here and there, it is mostly passive income.

You can also build entire businesses that are based on affiliate commissions. More on this in Chapter Six.

Services

Lastly, there are services. This is the least passive income model for blogging. Services require you to either work one-on-one with clients or with a group of clients. This can be things like running membership sites, conferences, mastermind calls, personal coaching, or other freelance type services, like design or social media management. Services can be a great way to earn a lot of income but they are more time consuming.

Using blogging to create multiple streams of income

The great thing about blogging is that you don't have to choose just one of these ways to earn money from your blog, you can choose to use all of them or just a few of these strategies. While it is pretty simple to start out using ads and affiliate income for blogging, adding digital products, sponsorships, and services takes a little more time to get things going. However, you can work on creating various income streams from your blog by incorporating different ways to earn income.

However, in order to earn any kind of income from your blog you need to get people to visit it first and become fans. You need to be able to find a large audience of readers who are willing to buy things from you, whether as an affiliate or things that you personally create.

WHERE YOU FIND YOUR AUDIENCE AND GET EYEBALLS ON YOUR SITE

When you first start a blog, actually getting traffic to your site and people to read your content can seem rather overwhelming with all the other blogs and websites already taking up their attention. If you don't understand how to market and how to use SEO to your advantage (we'll get to this in the next section), then it will be difficult for people to find you online.

Just as with many things in blogging, there are literally tons of different ways to get people to read your blog. The trick is to get them to read it and then buy something from you. Besides, the key here is to actually make a living from blogging.

There are many different ways to drive traffic to your site.

Just to name a few…

- Facebook posts
- Facebook ads
- Instagram posts
- Instagram ads
- Twitter posts
- SEO
- Pinterest pins
- Pinterest ads
- YouTube videos
- Adwords campaigns
- Backlinking

You see how this can get pretty confusing pretty quick?

Getting people to visit your site also depends on where your audience hangs out online. For example, if you are starting a food blog, Pinterest is a great place to start driving people to your website. If you are creating a blog on something that is already popular on a certain platform, use that platform to drive traffic to your blog.

Using social media to drive traffic

There are a few reasons why it's a great idea to use social media to start driving traffic to your blog. First of all, you don't have to buy ads, it's free (except for maybe paying automation software). Yes, you heard me right, it doesn't cost you anything to set up business accounts on Pinterest, Facebook, Twitter, Instagram or any other social network. You can post, as a blog/business, rather than using a personal account, and start getting traffic to your site.

SEO for traffic

Growing your blog using social media is great if you blog about topics that your friends and family would talk about or share on the various social media platforms (Marrow, 2019). These are topics like weight loss, health, parenting, DIY activities, or food. Using SEO is great for topics that people search for online. This can include product reviews (think "the best…"), how-to type information, or things you would ask an expert, like: "What is the best Wordpress plugin for creating a Table of Contents?"

Most likely, unless your friends and family are also bloggers, you are not going to be sitting around the table discussing Wordpress themes and plugins. This is where SEO is really going to give you a leg up. A good rule of thumb is to keep the posts on your site about 50/50. That is 50 percent on content that is highly shareable (list posts, how-tos, etc) while the other half should be searchable content (the best…).

Utilizing SEO is a great, and free, way to generate traffic to your site.

WHAT IS SEO AND WHY IT'S SO IMPORTANT

When you are just getting started with blogging the term SEO can be very intimidating. It can seem like this big magical thing that only the big dogs have a full understanding of. I can promise you, SEO is not as scary or difficult as you think. It is actually quite a simple process that anyone can learn in order to help bring traffic to their blog.

Moz, a very well known company that provides a high quality SEO tool, defines SEO as: "SEO stands for Search Engine Optimization. It's the practice of increasing both the quality and quantity of website traffic, as well as exposure to your brand, through non-paid (also known as 'organic') search engine results."

It is all about keywords. Many years ago, you could write a post and just keyword stuff, meaning that whatever keyword(s) you were trying to rank for you could just write it in the post a bunch of times. However, this didn't always make for great reading. This is when the search engines got smart. Search engines can now determine if you are writing a post simply to get ranked or to actually help your readers. If you are writing a post just to get it ranked, most likely you are not going to end up on the first page of Google. If you are writing your content with the intention of actually helping people, then there is a good chance that your articles will get ranked pretty high on Google's search results, which makes it easier for people to find you.

It also doesn't cost you anything to rank in Google, other than a lot of time and effort. You need to continually provide your audience with valuable and useful content that benefits your audience rather than just writing to get noticed by the search engines.

When you are writing your blog and focusing on search engine optimization, you need to understand user intent. There are three different kinds of user intent, those that are searching for information, those that are searching for a specific website, and those that are searching to purchase something.

In addition to understanding what the user intent for your audience is, you must also understand what your blog's goals are. Is your goal just to get people to sign up for your newsletter so you can market to them again later on, or are you looking to get them to buy something from you right away?

SEO really isn't a stand alone thing that you should be working towards on your blog, it is a means to a much bigger end. While using strategic SEO tactics can certainly help you to rank high on Google and other search engine results pages, just ranking on a search engine isn't going to help you unless people are clicking through to your site. In addition, it doesn't matter how many people are clicking through to your site but how many people are contributing to your larger business goals, such as buying something through an affiliate link.

While it is pretty awesome to see your site listed on the first page of Google, the bottom line, if it is not helping you to make money or achieve some other business goal, it's not doing you much good. The great thing about SEO is that you can continually work towards improving it on your site. It is fairly easy to see what your competitors are doing with their SEO strategies and to be able to learn from them in order to improve your SEO strategy.

If you are trying to get your blog ranked high in Google for something, search that term in Google and see what kinds of keywords are coming up in the autosuggest. When you figure out which of your competitors are ranking high for that specific keyword, then take a look at their site. How is the article structured? How are they using variations of the keyword(s) to get higher in the search rankings while still providing value to the audience? And most importantly, how can you do it better?

If the thought of SEO and all things related to search engines still scare you, don't worry, this is another area of your business that you can easily outsource.

CHAPTER SUMMARY

In its simplest form, a blog is an informational website made up of posts. All blogs are websites, but not all websites are blogs. Blogs are used by companies to help drive sales to their products and services.

Journaling blogs start out as personal blogs and then often develop into a business. Authority sites are very large, often cover a wider range of topics, and have teams of writers, editors, and people to manage the site. Niche blogs, while they can be large, focus on a more narrow topic.

Bloggers earn money in the following ways:

- Ads
- Sponsorships
- Digital products
- Affiliate sales
- Services

When blogging for business, you should always have a self-hosted site. This gives you more control over your site and how you can make money with it.

You can focus on one of the aforementioned revenue streams or you can use all of them to generate multiple streams of income from your blog.

There are many ways to get traffic to your blog:

- Facebook posts
- Facebook ads
- Instagram posts
- Instagram ads
- Twitter posts
- SEO
- Pinterest pins
- Pinterest ads
- YouTube videos
- Adwords campaigns
- Backlinking

You can drive traffic to your blog either through using social media or implementing SEO (Search Engine Optimization) tactics. The main thing to remember when you are working on a post and trying to optimize it for the search engines and your reader is user intent.

SEO is a means to a much larger end. You have to consider your blog's goals other than just trying to get on the first page of Google.

While it is good to have a solid understanding of SEO, you can also outsource to help drive more organic traffic to your blog.

CHAPTER RESOURCES

Where to sell digital products

- Shopify
- Etsy
- Clickbank

In the next chapter, I will reveal the secrets of making money on YouTube.

CHAPTER FIVE
YouTube Success Secrets Revealed

YOUTUBE HAS QUICKLY become a platform for entrepreneurs to make a great living. Just as with other digital nomad type business models available to those wanting to live the RV life, YouTube is a great option that offers flexibility while being able to build a fairly passive income business. People love watching videos and it is a landscape that is not going to change in the near future. While creating a YouTube channel on its own is great, it is also a great compliment for any kind of content creator - bloggers, freelancers, comedians, artists, and so on.

In this chapter, we are going to review how to get started on YouTube, an overview of creating your first video, how to grow your subscriber base so that you can monetize your channel, why you should document your RV adventures for your subscribers, how you can get paid actively and passively using this platform, and how you can use YouTube ads to generate a great passive income.

HOW TO GET STARTED WITH YOUTUBE

Getting started with YouTube is very easy, but just like with any other business you are both a creator and a business owner. As you are running a YouTube business you need to think of it *as a business* and have clear goals in mind. Really think about your goals before you jump into creating your channel. Do you just want to document your RV journey (also referred to as vlogging)? If so, what is going to make your channel unique and make people want to watch your videos?

Now, it's not to say that you need a channel that is totally unique, there are plenty of channels out there that document people traveling in their RV, but what about you or your channel is going to be able to give you an edge?

Take a look at other similar, popular channels that cover the same kinds of topics that you want to cover. What kinds of things do they cover in their videos? How are they branding themselves and their channels? What about the production of their videos? How can you come up with a channel that shows the true you (don't be fake!) and offers something different to your audience?

When starting your channel you don't need anything more than a good quality phone camera (which you probably already have) and a computer. You don't need to worry about fancy and expensive cameras to start with. Many successful YouTubers have started with just the bare minimum and worked their way up to bigger and better equipment once they actually started to make money.

Creating your YouTube channel takes a lot of practice to get started, especially if you are not used to being on camera. You have to be willing to mess up and let go of your control if you are going to grow, learn and improve. You are not going to become a master at YouTube overnight, it is going to take hours and hours of refining your video skills. You don't have to be perfect to start getting subscribers and to grow your channel.

The biggest thing that you are going to need to make your videos look good is great lighting. You can either do this with natural lighting, which shouldn't be too much of an issue if you are traveling around in your RV, or use a simple light from the store that has the ability to have multiple bulbs turned on at once. Just make sure that whatever equipment that you do have will be able to easily fit into your RV and will travel well.

Creating content

In the process of getting everything started, it is good to brainstorm a ton of different video ideas, at minimum 50-100 different ideas. With YouTube you need to be able to put out content on a consistent basis, whether it is a 5-minute video per day or one 30 minute video per week, you need to be prepared to create enough content. Out of all the different ideas that you come up with, start with the first 10 or so that you are really excited about and that you think will do well based on your previous research. You also need to figure out what your filming and upload schedule is going to be. It's better to focus on quality over quantity but also to be able to be consistent with your schedule (Perkins, 2108).

The actual creation of your YouTube channel is super simple, especially if you already have a Gmail account as they are linked. You are going to want to make sure that you have a banner for your channel and that you write a good description that is SEO friendly. This simply means write a description that really defines what your channel is actually about using words that your audience would search for. A channel banner and a good description help to make your channel look more professional and can encourage people to subscribe to your channel.

Creating your first video

Now onto the fun part, the actual video creation! Unless you already have experience in public speaking or have been an actor or actress, your first couple of videos are going to be a little awkward. It's OK! Go look at some of the first videos of your favorite YouTubers, I can bet you that they aren't very good. It is better to create the content and get it out there rather than to try and be a perfectionist about everything.

After you have done all the fun filming, it is time to edit the video and design your thumbnail. Again, people judge things by their cover. You need to create an eye-catching thumbnail that is going to get your audience's attention and make them want to click on the video. When it comes to editing your videos, choose an editing software that is easy to use. If you are not already familiar with how to edit videos this can be just another thing that can cause you to feel overwhelmed. There are many simple editing software out there. If you own a Mac you should already have iMovie installed, if you own a PC, there is Windows Movie Creator, which are both very user-friendly. For a very user-friendly and affordable video editor, Filmora is also a great option.

After you have edited and uploaded your first video (and every subsequent video after) it is beneficial to give your video a little boost. While this might sound a little funny, you should like your own video, give it a comment saying something like leave a comment below, and share your video wherever possible. This can include your Facebook page, your Instagram, your Twitter, and your Pinterest accounts. Don't be afraid to ask your friends and family to watch your video and like, and or, leave a comment. Every little bit of exposure that you can get in the beginning is going to help! By nature, the more views a video has the more people are going to watch it due to social proof.

The biggest thing is consistency! You need to be consistent in making your videos and uploading them. It is much easier to grow your channel if you are uploading videos on a regular basis rather than only uploading them once and awhile. While it can take anywhere from six to twelve months to actually start seeing a good amount of growth, having consistency and producing quality videos with eye-catching thumbnails is definitely going to help you.

GROWING YOUR SUBSCRIBER BASE

In order to actually make money from YouTube you need to have people watch your videos and subscribe to your channel. First of all, when you are making videos, ASK your audience to subscribe to your channel and to hit the like button.

Create awesome content

Just as with other online businesses you can turn to social media or use SEO tactics to drive traffic to your videos. There are a few components to building your subscriber base on your YouTube channel. You first must be able to create awesome content that is unique, valuable, interesting, and high quality.

Collaborate with influencers

The second part of being able to grow your audience very quickly is to get in front of other people's audiences. In the blogging world, this can be done through guest posting. In YouTube, it can mean collaborating with other YouTubers or social media influencers in a variety of ways. This can be done through being featured on another

YouTuber's video(s), being a guest on someone else's podcast, shout-outs on social media, and guest posting on their blog.

When you are reaching out to influencers to ask them to feature you, don't go after the big dogs. If you are just starting out it is likely that you will quickly get shut down. Go after influencers and other YouTubers that have a couple hundred or a couple thousand more followers than you do.

Remember, it's all about giving before you ask though. See what you can do for the blogger or YouTuber before you straight out ask them for something. People don't like that kind of stuff. As your audience grows, you can go after collaborating with influencers with bigger audiences. Keep in mind though, as you grow, reciprocate what others have done for you. Once your audience gets bigger and if someone asks you to collaborate, just remember what other influencers have done to help you out.

Quality over quantity

Before you even start reaching out to influencers you want to be sure that you are already creating stellar content. While there will always be vain people out there who only care about your follower count or number of views you have, more than likely they are going to care more about the type and quality of content you are putting out. Be sure that you are already providing your audience with a ton of value and are genuinely wanting to help people rather than just looking to inflate your numbers.

Now that you are ready to reach out to people and collaborate with them, it's time to start making a list. You are going to want to focus on people, again, that are just a few steps ahead of you, not miles. When you are reaching out to potential collaborators, make sure you actually have a pitch for them, rather than just asking them to help you without any sort of plan that also benefits them and their respective audiences.

Use other platforms to grow your subscribers

You can also look to social media to grow your subscriber base. If you already have an audience on platforms such as Pinterest, Facebook, Twitter, or Instagram, you can share your YouTube videos on your other profiles. Also make sure that you actually ask people to subscribe and like your videos when they are watching them on other channels as well.

Building your audience is going to take time and effort. Don't get discouraged when your numbers aren't going up the way you want them to.

Be authentic

It's important to remain authentic with your audience. If you are fake, sooner or later people are going to see through you and you won't have a very big or engaged audience for long. Don't forget to share your story with your audience as well. People love to hear how other people got started on their entrepreneurial journey.

You should also be consistent with your audience both online and offline. Your audience should feel that you are reliable in both your uploading schedule and your online personality.

Connecting with your community

In the process of building your community and after you have built up a really good following, you can't forget to connect with your community.

It's very important to connect with your audience, it not only benefits you as a creator but also benefits your community. Here are a few ways to connect with your audience:

Have conversations in the comments section

Remember when I mentioned before that you should comment on your own videos? This is not only a good practice to boost your videos but also to ask people to engage in the comments section. Make sure that you are promoting quality conversations in the comments section (Uhas, 2019) and responding to viewers' comments within the first few hours of them being posted. This lets viewers know that you care about their comments and appreciate that they are watching your videos. But make sure that you are only responding to actual comments that are meaningful and add value; don't respond to negative comments. Interacting with your audience in the comments section can also benefit you by providing useful information or suggestions and ideas for future videos.

Just as you would engage in the comments by commenting back, make full use of YouTube's tools and heart peoples' comments as well. This will, in turn, send them a notification letting them know that you have "hearted" their comments and that you, again, appreciate their contribution to your channel. Hearting a comment is something only the creator is allowed to do and shows a little something extra to your viewers.

Another really neat thing you can do in the comments section of your videos is to pin a comment to the top of the comments section. This allows for better engagement when you are asking your audience questions during your actual video. Your username in the comments is also surrounded by a little bubble of color, which helps to quickly indicate that you are an engaged creator.

Ask your audience for feedback

It's a great idea to also ask your audience for feedback. You don't have to worry about having a ton of views on your videos before you do this either. Pin a comment at the top of the comments section asking what your audience would like to see in upcoming videos. You can also do shout-outs to your audience in your videos. For example, "Today's video idea came from [viewer name]." This really helps to make your audience feel extra special and that you are really engaging with them.

There are a couple different ways that people can be notified of activity on your channel: by subscribing and by hitting the notifications bell. When they hit the notifications bell they are notified whenever you upload a new video.

Reward your superfans

There are two really fun ways that you can reward your superfans, those that watch EVERYTHING you put out and comment on all of your videos. You can make private videos or do livestreams. As a full-time RVer you could live stream taking your super audience on special adventures with you. This is also a great way to encourage regular audience members to become super members by bribing them with exclusive content.

Connect off of YouTube

Just because you are building a YouTube channel doesn't mean that you just have to stay on the YouTube platform. I previously mentioned being able to connect with other creators and your potential audience on other social media platforms. When you are first starting out and learning the ropes of everything, it is ok to stick to one channel. As your channel grows, expand your reach by using other social media channels.

The first thing to start with is promoting your videos on your other social media networks. Don't be afraid to do this a few times per week per video you are putting out. Videos that do really well on social media are the kinds of videos that are often funny, inspirational, or things that are very "Buzzfeed" inspired. So keep that in mind when you are creating your videos and sharing them on your various social media platforms.

Documenting your RV adventures for your subscribers

Think about this for a minute, if you have the dream of traveling around full time in an RV, do you watch videos on YouTube that inspire you or provide you with information on full-time RV living? I'm guessing you have watched at least a few. People love watching what others are doing and how they are achieving success and living their dreams. They find it inspirational as well as motivational.

Even if you start your YouTube channel before you officially start your RV adventure, there is no rule saying that you can only have one channel! People LOVE to watch videos on travel and traveling-tips. If you initially start a YouTube channel about something else, it is also a great idea to be able to document your RV adventures. Just do a quick search on "RV living" on YouTube and you can come up with a whole list of topics:

- RV remodels
- How much it really costs

- How to budget while being a full-time RVer
- Beginner mistakes that RVers make
- RV tours

Videos like these are getting TONS of views! So you can already see that there is an audience out there watching these videos.

GETTING PAID-ACTIVE AND PASSIVE INCOME IDEAS

While the goal of starting your YouTube channel is to make money, it is going to take a little bit to make that happen. Before you can start collecting checks from YouTube, you need to build an audience and make consistent content. Once you have a consistent stream of content and you are building up your audience, you can apply to the YouTube Partner Program to start actually monetizing your content. There are a couple of requirements that you need to meet before you can be accepted to the YouTube Partner Program:

- You need to be in good standing with YouTube
- Have at least 4,000 valid watch hours
- Have at least 1,000 subscribers

While this might sound like some big milestones to get started, if you follow the aforementioned tactics, you should be able to reach those milestones pretty quickly! However, it can take up to a month for YouTube to actually review and approve your channel, so keep that in mind. If for whatever reason your channel doesn't get approved, then you can reapply again in 30 days. In the meantime, read through YouTube's policies and see if there is something that you need to change in order to get approved. One of the main reasons that creators get removed from the Partner Program is if they are inactive for 6 months and fall below the qualification thresholds.

How you can actually generate revenue from ads

Once you have officially qualified for the YouTube Partner Program you can start to earn money from ads and from YouTube premium subscribers.

Ads are one of the most common ways that people make money on YouTube, specifically because there is a lower threshold to be able to make money from ads than from any other monetization strategy. But HOW you can make money from ads can be sort of confusing when you are just getting started.

After you have ensured that your content is advertiser friendly, you need to physically turn on ads on the platform. While YouTube does most of the heavy lifting when it comes to determining what type of ads are shown on your videos, there are a few ways that you can ensure that your audience will see relevant ads. YouTube determines which ads to put on videos based on your audience, the video-metadata, and if it is advertiser friendly.

There are several different kinds of ads that your videos can have. Display ads are shown to the right of your video and above the list of suggested videos. Overlay ads lay over the bottom 20% of the video that are semi-transparent. Bumper ads are those that the viewer can not skip and must watch the full ad before your video plays. There are also, of course, skippable ads as well as sponsored content that is relevant to your video. Finally, if your video is longer, there are mid-roll ads which play in the middle of the video.

Additional ways to earn money through YouTube

Recently, YouTube has been rolling out some new features for creators to earn additional income streams from their channels, such as memberships and super chat.

Memberships

YouTube memberships are only available for creators that have 100,000 subscribers and are over the age of 18 (sorry, no kids channels), and have already qualified for the YouTube Partner Program. Members can pay $4.99 per month to support the channel and get additional perks like badges and access to exclusive content in the community area of the channel.

Merchandise

YouTube has also added a merchandise feature. This is great news for creators as this can really help to increase their earnings. If the channel has 10,000 subscribers or more, YouTube creators can offer merchandise that shows up in a strip below their videos.

While there is really unlimited potential to this avenue, as a creator you should offer products that make sense to your audience. T-shirts are always a good place to start! *Hint: this is also why you should always create a brand from the beginning! YouTube has actually developed a partnership with TeeSpring to help initiate those sales. While obviously YouTube and TeeSpring have to take a cut of the sales, there is still plenty to be made.

Sponsorships

Creators can also land sponsored opportunities through FameBit.com. Sponsored opportunities are a great way to earn extra income on YouTube by connecting with much larger companies and promoting their products or services.

One really neat way to calculate how much money you can actually make from YouTube is to use the YouTube Money Calculator. You can also plug in a channel and it will show you approximately how much that channel is making. Just remember that you, the creator, only receive 55% of that total and you still need to pay taxes on those earnings as well. So if you live in the United States, take about another 30% away from your total. So out of every $100 you "make" on YouTube you only get to keep approximately $38.50.

What you need to know about YouTube ads

I've mentioned a few times about creating content that is advertiser-friendly, but what does this actually mean? First of all, what you need to realize is that not every video uploaded to YouTube is manually reviewed but rather initially reviewed by an algorithm. Sometimes this algorithm doesn't have enough information from the video for it to determine if it adheres to YouTube's advertiser friendly guidelines. In this case, it might get demonetized.

But fear not!

You can always request a manual review if you feel that you are adhering to the guidelines. The thumbnail, description, and the title of your video can have a huge impact. It should not have any swear words, anything racy, and the thumbnail, description, and title should all be directly relevant to the video itself.

What NOT to make videos about

Some of the topics that advertisers find off-limits are issues such as school shootings, terrorism, death, sexual abuse, and any kind of related topics. The bottom line is you can certainly make videos on these topics, but many advertisers just don't want to be associated with those kinds of topics, therefore those types of videos will likely be demonetized.

Topics that revolve around drugs or substance abuse can be monetized but ONLY if they are education-based and not promoting the use, abuse, or sale of such substances. Advertisers can also choose to be shown on videos that include potentially sensitive drug material.

Videos that also include potentially physical and emotional harm to another person can also be a little iffy as to whether they are able to be monetized. Prank videos are a perfect example of this. While prank videos can certainly be monetized, and many people make a good living doing these types of videos, it should be shown in the video that the individual that is getting pranked is not seriously injured.

Swearing and profanity can be a big cause of having videos demonetized. While it is certainly ok to drop a swear word here and there in your videos, bleep them if possible. Leave them out of the title, description, and thumbnail. The context of the swearing also has a lot to do with whether or not your videos will be monetized or not. If it is mean-spirited, then it is likely that your video will be flagged. However, if you are saying it as a reaction to something then that is generally acceptable.

Realistically, there are various kinds of content that advertisers don't want their ads running on. If you are unsure if your content is advertiser-friendly, you can always reference YouTube's Advertiser-Friendly Guidelines. This goes into the various different categories that advertisers don't want their ads running on as well as limited ads based on the nature of the content.

CHAPTER SUMMARY

Getting started with YouTube is very easy. You don't need anything other than a smartphone camera and a computer to start your channel.

Make sure to do your research and take a look at other popular channels in the same niche and what kind of content they are creating.

Don't be afraid to mess up. Start with what you have, use natural light whenever possible. If you are looking at video equipment, take the smaller size of an RV into consideration before making your purchase.

Come up with a consistent content schedule for recording, editing, and uploading.

Again, try not to be a perfectionist here. It's better to create your content with a less than perfect setup and get it out there than to not do anything at all.

Give your video an initial boose by commenting, liking, and sharing it on other platforms. This also helps to increase your social proof, so the more views it has, the more views it will get.

Consistency is key! Be consistent in uploading your videos even though it might take six to twelve months to see the growth you desire.

Often an overlooked aspect to driving growth on your channel is to actually ask people to like, subscribe, and hit the notifications bell.

Grow your channel through collaborating with other YouTubers and influencers. Always make sure that you are providing your viewers with high quality and valuable content.

Connect with your audience through the comments section, asking for feedback, and by rewarding your superfans. You can also connect with your audience outside of YouTube on other social media platforms like Facebook and Twitter.

While you can certainly start a channel about something else before you start out on your RV adventures, there is nothing wrong with having two channels.

Make sure that you understand all of YouTube's policies so that you are more likely to get approved to monetize using ads. YouTube does all the heavy lifting when it comes to which ads to run on your videos.

YouTube creators can also earn money through memberships and merchandise when they meet additional qualifications. Creators can also work with sponsors to create additional revenue streams.

You should always make sure that you are adhering to YouTube's advertiser guidelines so you can continue to monetize your videos. In order for your videos to remain monetized, ensure that you stay away from topics that involve drugs, sex, school shootings, terrorism, sexual abuse, physical violence, death, profanity, and all that other bad stuff.

CHAPTER RESOURCES

Video editors

- iMovie
- Windows Movie Creator
- Filmora

YouTube resources

- FameBit.com - for sponsorship opportunities
- YouTube Money Calculator - check out how much your favorite channels are making!
- YouTube's Advertiser-Friendly Guidelines

In the next chapter, we are going to cover how to build a sustainable business using affiliate marketing.

CHAPTER SIX
The Secrets To Affiliate Marketing Only The Pros Know

AFFILIATE MARKETING IS a great way to start your online journey. There are hundreds, if not thousands of online millionaires that either started as affiliate marketers or are still doing affiliate marketing, at least in some capacity.

There are also some very good opportunities to earn affiliate commissions on a passive income basis.

In this chapter, we are going to take a look at what affiliate marketing actually is, the best companies to use to start your affiliate marketing journey, how affiliate marketers earn money, why it's easier to sell other people's products, and if you need a website to get started!

WHAT IS AFFILIATE MARKETING?

Some of the biggest names in online business got started with affiliate marketing and learning how to generate passive income.

The Golden Goose, the American Dream...

To make money while you sleep!

The basic premise of affiliate marketing is that you promote other peoples' products and earn a commission when someone buys a product through your link. Sounds pretty easy right?

Within the affiliate marketing model there are three main components: the advertiser, the publisher, and the customer. The advertiser is the person or company whose products you are promoting. As an affiliate marketer, you are the publisher. Finally, the customer is just that, the person who is buying the product or service.

As an affiliate, it is your job to convince the customer to buy the product or service so that you get paid a commission. But the customer actually needs to buy something in order for that to happen. You can promote affiliate offers through your own review website, social networks, email marketing, or even ads (if that is ok with the advertiser). The great thing about affiliate marketing is that the price of the actual products or services doesn't increase just because the affiliate is earning a commission.

You can find merchants or advertisers either through affiliate networks or as an individual company or solopreneur. Affiliate networks offer a wide range of affiliate products to choose from, often from many different categories. Some merchants choose only to go through an affiliate network to manage their affiliates.

You can also become an affiliate for more than one company. Then there are the affiliate programs for solopreneurs or other small business owners. This often includes being an affiliate for a limited number of products, such as the creator's course or ebook.

It really doesn't matter what niche you want to cover, there is a related affiliate program out there to promote. There are thousands of affiliate products for B2B and B2C. By far, one of the biggest and most well known affiliate programs out there is the Amazon

Associates program. It is easy to apply to and you don't even need a website to get accepted.

THE BEST AFFILIATE COMPANIES TO JOIN

There are thousands, if not millions of affiliate programs that you could join. But the good news is that you don't need to worry about joining a thousand different affiliate programs. There is one in particular that does a great job for just about any niche you are in, as well as a few really good runner ups.

Amazon Associates

Amazon is the best affiliate program to join when you are first starting out. Not only is Amazon Associates great for those that are just starting out, huge companies like Buzzfeed and the New York Times use Amazon's affiliate program to monetize their sites. In the United States alone, 49% of ALL online sales can be attributed to Amazon. That is HUGE!

People are making hundreds and thousands of dollars per month just from the Amazon Associates program and there doesn't seem to be any slowing down.

Bloggers and business owners love using the Amazon Associates program for many reasons. One of the biggest things is that Amazon is so big that you can find just about any product on there that will fit in with your niche.

From baby products to some pretty weird and crazy stuff like a bag of air (seriously, I'm not even joking about this!), there are bound to be products in your niche. Even better, more than likely, you are bound to find something that your audience will want to buy. Amazon is also pretty old in internet terms, which is a good thing. It has such an incredible knowledge of its customers and gets an insane amount of traffic every day.

There are, however, a couple of downfalls about the Amazon Associates program to take into consideration.

First, it is mostly for physical products, other than eBooks. So if you are looking to promote other people's digital programs, Amazon can't help much with that, although who knows what the future will bring. If you want to promote a mix of both physical and digital products you can supplement your Amazon affiliate income with Clickbank products.

Amazon can also be pretty strict, which can make it difficult for some people to follow their terms of service. Just make sure that you are thoroughly reading Amazon's Terms of Service and understanding them so you don't get yourself into trouble. While you can make a lot from Amazon, there are some niches where commissions are much lower than others, so take that into account when you are picking which products to promote.

There are a ton of benefits to using the Amazon Associates program. We already know how big it is and just about everyone has heard of Amazon. This means the trust factor is already there and you don't have to worry about convincing people to buy. Because of the trust factor, the conversions for Amazon are pretty high. There are tons of different ways in which you can promote Amazon affiliate products.

Lastly, you have the option to transition to the Amazon FBA program (more on this in the next chapter). Amazon has also become a master at upselling their customers, which benefits you as you earn a commission on anything that customer buys within 24 hours after clicking on your link.

HOW EXACTLY DO AFFILIATES EARN MONEY?

Amazon is a little different than other affiliate programs out there. Similar to other programs, when someone clicks on your link and are taken to the Amazon site, they are tagged with your special code that attributes the sale (and commission) to you. The neat thing about the Amazon Associates program is that once they click on your link, whatever they buy from Amazon in the next 24 hours, you get a commission for. This means, if they click your link to buy a $2.99 eBook, and then decide to purchase a new $800 tv within the next 24 hours, you get the commission.

There are several ways that you can earn money from Amazon by promoting their products. If you are recommending a certain product, you simply link the product. You can do this by talking about the product in a blog post and simply linking to it through what is called an anchor text. This simply means that you use keywords of the product in the text and link to the product.

You can also use what are called native shopping ads. You can create these native ads, which look like other regular ads, for individual products within categories of products. This is great to use to stack on top of other Amazon revenue streams. For example, if you are making a post about Instant Pot recipes, you can place a native ad in the post that links to certain Instant Pot accessories.

Did you know that 60% of Amazon's sales come from mobile users? Which is why mobile popover ads can be so beneficial to add Amazon revenue to your passive income streams.

Once someone has clicked on your link and been taken to Amazon, they make a purchase. In order for you to get a payout, the purchase needs to be completed and delivered. If they make a return, you don't get a commission.

You can get paid out via direct deposit with as little as $10, or if you prefer old fashioned checks, then you have to wait until you have accumulated at least $100 in affiliate commissions. Depending on the product, you can earn between 1%-10% affiliate commission on products. There are certain things that don't pay out a commission either, such as gift cards, wireless service plans, digital Kindle products, alcoholic beverages, and a few others.

The actual sign up process is super simple and only takes a few minutes. Almost anyone can easily get approved to start promoting affiliate products through Amazon.

Getting people to click on your links

So you know how to get links to products and use ads to promote Amazon products, but what about actually getting people to click on your links? It's not as complicated as it sounds. There are a couple of different ways to promote your Amazon links and start earning an income from them!

If you already have a blog or are thinking of starting one, then roundup posts are a great place to start putting in your affiliate links. You have most likely already seen these online and have read a few of them yourself. These types of posts often target "the best" kinds of products to drive sales of the product.

When writing a roundup post, be careful though, Amazon is very particular about how much of their content you can use within your post. For example, you should not use their ratings but rather ensure that your reader knows that the ratings you are including (if you are including ratings) are all your own opinion.

A traditional roundup is meant to act as a buying guide to help customers make informed buying decisions. Including product reviews can be very helpful here. But again, watch out when you are taking information from Amazon. Don't just use the product description but rather share with your readers why you are recommending the product to them.

There are also roundup listicles, which are very similar to the traditional roundup post. Roundup listicles are more shopper-centric and are easier for readers to browse without having to read too much if they don't want to. These often link to the Amazon full reviews rather than reviewing the product itself. The big downfall with this is that smaller sites shouldn't do it. Google doesn't exactly like sites that are JUST affiliate links and no actual education or information for the reader.

The last kind of roundup that is great for promoting your affiliate links is the "clear winner" roundup. This helps to take some of the guesswork out of which product the buyer should purchase by giving them a "clear winner" or "editor's choice." While this is technically a roundup post, most of the content will focus on the best product (*Hint, which is often the most expensive one, which gets you a higher commission) while briefly mentioning other, comparable products.

Then there are single product reviews. These are just a post on a review of a single product rather than several. The great thing about roundups and product reviews is that there is buying intent behind these searches. It all comes down to the psychology of sales.

Think for a minute, before you make a purchase, often a larger purchase, you might look for product reviews to determine which product to purchase. Think of keyword phrases like "the best running shoes," or "the best recumbent bikes," generally speaking if you are looking up phrases like these then you are about ready to buy something rather than just doing more research. With writing a single product review you need to go into a little more depth on the actual product and not just rehash some information from Amazon.

A versus post is taking two products and comparing the pros and cons to each other. Rather than giving your readers only one choice, or a whole host of options, they only have to choose between two options. This can be very helpful for those that are rather indecisive.

People often do this comparison by themselves anyways. When they have narrowed down on their search results and have picked two products but can't seem to decide on one or the other they will often search "*[product A] versus [product b]*." If they can find a post of exactly the two products they are looking for that will help to build trust in that source, which is you.

Finally, there are tutorials and problem solving content. Generally speaking, there is urgency associated with someone looking online for a tutorial or something to help them solve an issue. When someone is in need of something to help them solve a problem this can drastically help with conversions as well.

Often times tutorial type posts don't even need to focus on the product that much and can just provide it as a solution to the audience. Think of posts that start with things like: "*The benefits of...,*" "*How to...,*" and "*X# of ways to...*"

You can easily put in Amazon affiliate links into any post by searching Amazon and using the Site Stripe once you have signed up for a business account. The Site Stripe is just a bar that goes across the top of your Amazon business account. Once you type in a product and click on the individual product you can link via a short link, a long link, using just an image, or using an image and text.

It is recommended that you do use the full affiliate link rather than the shortened version, this can assist in making the transition to change the links in the future much easier.

There are also several other ways to build links from Amazon into your website or blog, which include the Amazon Publisher Studio, the Amazon Link Builder Plugin for WordPress, and OneLink. All of these offer their own advantages and can be used to easily change links should the need arise.

While there are plenty of places where you can promote Amazon affiliate links, there are places in which you can not. Doing so will likely get your account deleted and there goes all of your commissions along with it! Here are a few things that you need to make sure you have in place and that you DON'T do when you are trying to earn money through Amazon affiliate links.

- Always have a disclaimer on your site.

This can be either on each individual post, in the footer, or sidebar. But you need to make sure that it is very clear to your audience that you earn a commission from Amazon if someone makes a purchase through your link.

- Don't download images from Amazon and use them on your site.

This is a big no-no! If you reference Amazon's Terms of Service, the wording on this is sort of vague. But it is always better to err on the side of caution when it comes to using images. You can, however, use the images that are available through the Site Stripe.

- Whatever Amazon images you do use MUST link back to the product on Amazon.
- You can not promote Amazon products via email.

This does not mean that you can't write a post about a product and link to that post within the email. Again, better safe than sorry here.

- You can not promote any Amazon products by using pop-up ads.
- You can't put the price out there.

Unfortunately, many people still do this and are unknowingly violating the Terms of Service. For example, if you are promoting a product you can not place a button under it stating the price. You can, however, place a button that says something like, *"Click here to check price,"* or *"Buy Now,"* or *"Check Amazon for Lowest Price."* These are all great options that still encourage people to click through without violating the Terms of Service. The only time that you can directly mention the price of an item on Amazon is when you link to the API. This helps to pull the most recent price directly from Amazon so you aren't intentionally or unintentionally misleading your customers with a false price. You can also use vague dollar symbols in place of actual prices.

- Don't try and get your friends and family to buy stuff through your links.

Amazon is SMART! They can tell if you are just sending people links to get them to buy stuff so you can generate a commission. This is one sure way to get your account shut down. Customers must click on your link through a natural buying process and can't be forced.

- You can share your links on social media.

The only stipulation is that you need to add your social media profiles to your list of approved sites with Amazon. Then you are good to go!

Other Affiliate Networks to Consider

In addition to using Amazon as an affiliate platform there are a few others that are worth considering:

- Clickbank-Great for digital products in a wide variety of niches.
- Rakuten-Affiliate platform for places like Target, Walmart, and Kohl's.
- eBay Partner Program-for everything available on eBay!
- ShareASale-Great if you are planning on doing B2B, lots of business-related products.
- FlexOffers-Some featured advertisers include CreditSesame and Overstock.com.
- GiddyUp-This is a great platform for those affiliates that are looking to get into highly specific or more obscure niches.
- JVZoo-This program offers a lot of software-based and digital products.
- CJ Affiliate by Conversant-A HUGE name in affiliate marketing, some of their advertisers include GoPro, Barnes and Noble, and Priceline.
- Avangate-A great option if you want to promote software products (Edwards, 2018).
- MarketHealth-Great for health and beauty products.

While some offers are only available on certain affiliate platforms, there are some businesses that are affiliated through multiple platforms. In this case, make sure to do your research to see which one pays out higher commissions or has more affiliate resources. Heck, some affiliate platforms even let you become an affiliate, meaning that if someone becomes an affiliate for that platform you can then make money off of their commissions too!

One thing to keep in mind when you are choosing which affiliate network to start working with is that digital and software products often have higher commission payouts than physical products.

WHY IT'S BETTER TO SELL OTHER PEOPLE'S PRODUCTS

While Amazon is a great affiliate platform to use, wouldn't you make more money if you just made your own products?

Well, yes and no…

You could certainly spend months developing a product, working with suppliers from overseas, creating an entire marketing plan around your ONE product.

OR…

You would simply hook up with other merchants and use their products. This is a lot less work on your part and you can start generating cash a lot quicker and with a lot less investment in both time and money.

While creating your own product can be highly profitable, it can be rather pricey and labor intensive to get started. When you use other people's products there is already proven success that people buy those products, otherwise they probably wouldn't be on Amazon in the first place.

With many kinds of affiliates, they often have full campaigns in place. This can include product landing pages, email newsletter templates, video sales letters, and long-form sales letters that these companies often pay hundreds of thousands of dollars to initially get set up.

So it is not only free for you to start making money through affiliate links, there is a whole host of resources that you are able to use to help drive sales. The more sales you are able to drive to the product, the more money you make, and the more money the merchant makes. It's really a win-win for everyone involved.

DO YOU ACTUALLY NEED A WEBSITE TO BE AN AFFILIATE?

There are plenty of affiliates who got their start without a website. However, there is a lot more you can do if you have your own site. It can vary drastically from merchant to merchant and from network to network. Some affiliate networks won't even let you sign up if you don't already have a website that has content that they can approve.

Let's take Amazon and Clickbank for example. You don't technically need a website to share affiliate links. You can "microblog," simply meaning that you are putting an affiliate link in a very small post on social media in order to promote it.

Some other affiliate networks will require you to have a website, such as FlexOffers. Often times this helps merchants to see how you will be promoting their products. Even if you are accepted into an affiliate network, you might also need to apply to every individual merchant. If for whatever reason you get denied, there should be an explanation in which you can work to resolve the issue and apply again for approval.

The biggest piece of advice that I have when it comes to affiliate marketing is to choose one niche to focus on. It can be very tempting when you see the potential to make a lot of money from all the different affiliate networks out there to want to do them all. Do your best to avoid shiny object syndrome and focus on one, at least in the beginning.

Affiliate marketing is also a great passive income tool. There are so many things that you can outsource and automate once you get your systems up and running. Of course, the more passive income you are able to generate the better!

CHAPTER SUMMARY

Many online millionaires have started their journey with affiliate marketing. Affiliate marketing is also a great passive income model.

The basic idea of affiliate marketing is that you set up a site or put links out online and when people buy through those links you earn a commission.

In an affiliate marketing relationship there is the advertizer, the publisher (that's you), and the customer. You can promote affiliate links through your website, social media accounts, email list, and even ads. You earn a commission all while the customer does not have to worry about a price increase.

There are many different affiliate platforms and marketplaces to choose from. Be sure to understand each program's terms of service.

Amazon pays you a commission on everything the customer buys within 24 hours of clicking on your link. You can earn a commission from Amazon through affiliate links, native shopping ads, and mobile pop over ads.

You can drive traffic to your links through roundup posts, review posts, buying guides, and roundup listicles. Make sure you are not just filling your site with affiliate links and that it has some educational content as well.

When you are writing your post, keep the buyer intent in mind. When linking to Amazon products, it is recommended to use the full link rather than the shortened version.

There are a few things that you need to make sure that you do (and don't do) when promoting Amazon affiliate links:

- Have a disclaimer on your site.
- Don't use images directly from Amazon.
- You can use Site Stripe images.
- Any image should link back to the Amazon product.
- You can't promote products directly through email.
- You can't use pop-up ads.
- You can't advertise the price unless linked with API.
- Don't bribe your friends and family to buy stuff through your links.
- You can share your links on social media.

Digital and software products often have higher payouts than physical products. It is also a lot easier to get started selling other peoples' products than to start off selling your own.

There are many affiliate networks available that you don't even need a website to get started with.

CHAPTER RESOURCES
Affiliate companies/platforms

- Amazon Associates
- Clickbank
- Rakuten
- eBay Partner Program
- ShareASale
- FlexOffers
- GiddyUp
- JVZoo
- CJ Affiliate by Conversant
- Avangate
- MarketHealth

In the next chapter, we are going to cover the essentials you need to successfully start an Amazon FBA business.

CHAPTER SEVEN
Essential Amazon FBA Tactics To Grow Your Business

Did you know that there are over 2 million people selling products on Amazon? You might not realize it but Amazon is very similar to eBay in that just about anyone can list things for sale on Amazon. It doesn't matter if you purchased the item wholesale, made it yourself, or it was something you were going to put in a garage sale.

In this chapter, we are going to cover all the essentials of getting started with Amazon FBA. This includes what FBA actually is, how you can select a winning product or products that people are willing to pay for, where to find these products, how FBAs actually make money, and how to run Amazon ads to drive traffic to your products.

WHAT IS AMAZON FBA?

While you can fulfill orders you receive on Amazon personally, there is an easier way, especially if you have a lot of products. This is where Amazon FBA, or Fulfillment By Amazon, comes in really handy! You can get your product, ship it to Amazon, they keep it stored in their warehouse, and they will take care of the rest. This includes packing, shipping, and even returns.

You can see why so many people find this to be an attractive business model.

This is particularly attractive to someone living the RV lifestyle as you don't have to worry about carting around inventory, packing materials, or finding the nearest UPS to ship out your orders.

Once all the initial leg work is done, there is a lot less to worry about on a regular basis than if you were personally handling all of the orders.

One of the advantages of selling on Amazon through FBA is that your products are available for Amazon Prime. Considering Amazon Prime members spend almost twice the amount annually on Amazon purchases, there is a huge market of buyers just waiting to purchase your product(s).

In addition to handling pretty much everything once Amazon receives your products (there sometimes might be minimal customer service involved), you get paid every two weeks! No having to wait three months before ever seeing a check. As long as you are making sales, this creates reliable and consistent income, which is great when you are living on the road!

Starting your FBA business

So what does it take to get set up with Amazon FBA anyhow?

It does take some work to get started selling on Amazon through FBA. First, you need to choose a product to sell - sometimes this is easier said than done. This is where a lot of people get hung up and quit before they ever even get started.

We will focus on how to pick a winning product in the next section.

If you are going to be using FBA (which is the goal here!) then pick a product that is going to sell fast. This way you are turning a profit quickly and won't have to worry about paying Amazon storage fees.

The next step is to keep your inventory stocked. While this is a simple task, it is very important. If you are constantly running out of stock you are going to lose customers and Amazon will be less likely to show your listing to potential customers.

Lastly, and this is the biggest upkeep part, is the advertising and marketing of your products. With hundreds of millions of products on Amazon you need to be sure that your product doesn't get buried and people actually see it and buy it.

The challenges and benefits of Amazon FBA

If you are leaning towards starting an Amazon FBA business, there are some things to take into consideration before you jump in feet first.

It can cost a bit to get started with Amazon FBA. In addition to paying for the actual products, which can cost thousands of dollars initially, there are Amazon service fees and fulfilment fees.

There is also the potential to pay storage fees if your inventory sits in the warehouse for too long. Amazon wants to sell your products just as much as you do, however, if your products are sitting in their warehouse for six-months or more, you are going to be charged a pretty penny for it.

While having Amazon Prime is great and it can make returns for customers super easy, that isn't always good for you. Making things easy to return means that impulse buys are more likely to be returned; it happens. After awhile you should be able to see a trend in your product sales and returns and be able to predict your potential loss for returns.

Amazon is a well oiled machine for a reason, they are very particular with how they want things done. You need to have your items properly prepared and shipped to the right warehouse. While this might take some time to get the hang of, once you know how to do it, it shouldn't be very difficult.

As I said before, you need to be able to keep up on your inventory so you don't run out and lose customers. It can be difficult to track inventory and sync everything up. However, there are automated apps and software that help to alleviate this annoyance.

And then there are taxes...

Nobody likes taxes, they are a pain in the butt, and vary by state and country. But again, there are solutions to help automate the tax process so you don't get hung up with this.

The benefits of selling through Amazon FBA

While there certainly is a learning curve with Amazon FBA, and it can be rather intimidating for people to get started, there are certainly numerous benefits!

There are so many amazing things about selling through Amazon FBA. Without having to manage your own fulfillment you can save a ton of time and stress. Having to fill your own orders is very time consuming, not to mention, takes up a lot of space, which you don't have if you are living full-time in an RV. If you are selling a lot of products, that means more space you need and more time spent fulfilling the orders.

You don't have to worry about outrageous shipping costs either. Amazon has partnered with some of the biggest shipping carriers to offer its FBA members a huge discount on shipping costs (Carragher, 2018). The customer benefits also as there as several ways to get free shipping, such as through a Prime membership as well as purchasing qualified items, generally spending $25 or more.

Amazon FBA also handles all of your returns. Amazon handles everything, for a small processing fee. This can include handling upset customers, all the admin tasks that go along with it, customer inquiries, return and shipping labels, 24-hour customer phone support, and so on. While there is a charge for this, it is definitely worth it to make your business more passive.

Unlike other businesses that require certain amounts of inventory, there is no minimum for Amazon FBA, you can even send them just one product. You also pretty much have unlimited storage potential. This is great news if you are just testing the waters, and also if you are rapidly expanding. And the best part? You don't have to worry about your inventory taking up any space in your RV!

With Amazon's nationwide reach, there should be no problem getting customers their products quickly. Now, some Prime members can get their products in a day! Amazon also offers Multi-Channel Fulfillment, which means that you can sell your Amazon product on other platforms, such as BigCommerce, and Amazon will still work to fulfill those orders, pretty neat!

HOW TO SELECT WINNING PRODUCTS THAT SELL!

This is another area where people can really get hung up. They realize that they NEED products to sell. They might have an idea as to what to sell. However, they can be so overwhelmed at the same time that they end up picking the wrong thing or never even bother getting started.

There are literally millions of things that you could choose to sell online, from sponges to supplements and everything in between. While many people can handle figuring out the logistics and the marketing aspects of Amazon FBA, the part of the business that includes picking out a product to sell is downright scary! What if you pick the wrong thing? What if it doesn't sell? What if the market is too saturated?

Believe me, everyone that started Amazon FBA has had the same fears and questions. The difference between people that consistently doubt themselves and the ones that actually make a good living online doing Amazon FBA is confidence!

Once they have chosen their products, they are confident in their sales process that they are going to make enough money to support themselves and their business. While picking the wrong product can waste you a lot of time and money (which nobody wants) picking a product that sells can help to exponentially grow your business.

While products themselves are important, the niche(s) you pick to promote hold just as much clout. People often think that they have to start with picking a product before they pick a niche, this is simply not true. You should pick a niche before you dive into product research.

Even with really good research and picking a profitable niche, it is likely that your first product won't be a total hit. There is a lot of trial and error when it comes to Amazon FBA.

When it comes to picking a niche, it is better to go narrower than wider. As the saying goes, the riches are in the niches. The great thing about hyper-focused niches in that the customers in those niches are super passionate. Take road biking for example. While there are lots of people that like to ride their bikes, road biking or cycling is a hyper-focused niche. Cyclists spend a lot of money on their bikes and accessories. Amazon does a great job of catering to this by placing their products in categories, which gives you an advantage for finding a niche (Bryant, 2014). Here is an example of what I mean:

Home, Garden & Pets > Pet Supplies > Houses & Habitats > Accessories > Aquarium Décor > Plastic Plants

Your niche then would be aquarium decor and or plastic plants.

Now that you have a general idea on how to pick a product, what about *actually* picking a product? If you have some ideas on products you would like to sell but still aren't sure where to start, JungleScout is your best option. JungleScout is a software and Chrome browser extension that will help you to pick winning products over and over again! JungleScout can help you to find profitable products, track product sales, get details on Amazon search data, research quality suppliers, improve your advertising campaigns, optimize your listings to increase buyers, launch new products, and send automated emails to your customers. In addition, with the Chrome browser extension, you can get an insight into instant sales estimates, evaluate a product's revenue potential, validate product demand, and analyze the competition. Basically, if you aren't using JungleScout to help you run your Amazon FBA business, you are leaving a lot to chance.

WHERE CAN I FIND PRODUCTS TO SOURCE?

The vast majority of people first getting started with Amazon FBA start by importing their products from China. The biggest reason for this is because they are cheap and the profit margins are generally higher. However, there is a rather large learning curve that goes along with importing from overseas.

The two most common sites to use to import products from China are Alibaba and AliExpress. Aliexpress is great if you just want to order a few different products to get started with to test the waters without having to commit to a larger wholesale orders. You can order even one product at a time to get a feel for the quality and customer service when working with China wholesalers.

Alibaba, on the other hand, you have to place wholesale orders with. While some minimum orders can be as small as two pieces, there are many that require you to order hundreds of pieces of product at a time. When placing a wholesale order with Alibaba, you will also receive a discount on pricing the more you order. While this is generally a few cents per unit, that can really add up when you are ordering hundreds of units.

When you begin working with a supplier, you should ask for samples to ensure that you are getting a good quality product. Most often, suppliers are more than willing to work with a buyer (that's you) to provide you with a product that you will keep buying from them. Suppliers can also alter products to your specifications, such as creating different colors or adding your logo on the product to make it stand out from the millions of other products on Amazon. It is better to go through a few rounds of samples to ensure you are getting exactly what you want rather than worrying about upsetting the supplier and having to pay for a huge order that is going to get bad reviews.

Why you should outsource from overseas

Other than generating high profit margins, there are several other reasons why you should consider placing your wholesale orders from a wholesaler in China.

It is actually very easy to import items from China to America. With some items it is actually cheaper to ship from China to the U.S. rather than to ship within the U.S. This is because the U.S. Postal Service and China sellers actually have deals to highly cut the cost of shipping items that are under one pound.

You don't have to worry about traveling to China to see your products that you are selling (Bryant, 2018), although you certainly can travel to China. *Bonus-that's a tax deduction! So why not go see your products and the wholesaler factory up close and personal while also enjoying a fun and relaxing vacation?

When you are working with wholesalers in China, you don't have to settle for standard off-the-shelf products. You can actually work with them to develop a product from scratch or improve upon an existing product. Being able to actually develop a real, tangible product from scratch is fun and exciting. Even if it's a small product, there really isn't anything better than holding that real product in your hands for the first time!

While you might think that you are too late to the game, don't worry, you aren't!

Amazon has been growing and will continue to grow in the future. Just look around you. How many stores, even larger chains, close their doors because they haven't been getting enough business? The trend of online shopping isn't going to be slowing down any time soon. People are always looking for new products and ways to improve their lives with things they buy on Amazon.

While this might sound like an expensive endeavor, it is what you make of it. Many people have started their Amazon FBA businesses with only a few hundred dollars. Although it is ideal to be able to start with a few thousand dollars to allow for a little more wiggle room with testing. You must also have an Amazon Seller Central account which will cost you about $40 a month.

A word of caution though.

You should look into becoming an LLC rather than just a sole proprietor. Whenever you are dealing with products, there is always the potential for something to go wrong. A kid could swallow something, customers could misuse the product and somehow become injured. It happens. If you are a sole proprietor you can personally be sued for damages and lose everything that you have built.

However, if you establish an LLC, you personally can not he held liable for any damages. You are then a separate entity from your business. So take this into consideration when you are budgeting everything when starting out.

CASHING IN: HOW TO MAKE MONEY WITH AMAZON FBA

Now that we have covered what it takes and how much it costs to get started, it's time to talk about what everyone wants to know. How much money can you make with Amazon FBA.

The short answer is...

There is no guarantee. There are two main things to consider when you talk about how much you can make from selling on Amazon with FBA. There is the revenue and the profit. If you have ever watched a webinar or read an article about how much people make with Amazon FBA, they often talk about the revenue. Things like, *"I made $115,000 in sales last month,"* or *"Our store generated over a million dollars last year!"*

While these numbers are meant to inspire people to start their own Amazon FBA business, they are not entirely true. Revenue is how much people paid to buy the product. This is NOT how much you are actually putting into your pocket.

There are things like the cost of inventory, brokerage fees, freight fees, inspection fees, paying contractors, and of course, Amazon has to take their cut. Now the actual profit margins (the percentage you actually make from the product after all the fees come out) can be anywhere between 10-60%.

This is a very wide range but really depends on your product and what you are spending money on. If you are buying ads, that is another expense. However, purchasing ads can drastically increase the traffic to your listing and drive sales up.

So when you are hearing people talk about how much they make from Amazon, just remember that they are generally talking about revenue. There aren't too many people out there that talk about what their profit margins are and how much they are actually putting back in their pockets.

THE ESSENTIALS OF RUNNING AMAZON ADS

It seems like every platform has their own ads. Facebook, Twitter, Google, Instagram, and now Amazon. Implementing Amazon ads can be a great tool to help grow your business much quicker. There are a few tactics that you should be aware of to help your Amazon ads gain traction from the very beginning.

- Sponsored brands help to build brand awareness

When a potential customer is searching for a product, they will be served with the sponsored ads first as they appear above the products. This will immediately help to promote brand awareness for your product. If customers are searching for similar products and your product keeps coming up, they are likely to recognize it.

- Sponsored products should use category-specific targeting

Sponsored products are slightly different than sponsored brands as they appear above, below, and along the side of the search results in Amazon. The great thing about sponsored products is that Amazon pairs your product alongside similar products within a category, which can greatly increase your chances of making a sale. You, as the advertiser, are then able to pick if your product is shown next to certain brands or other specific products. This can be extremely helpful when you are trying to target customers that already buy certain products from a certain brand. This is known as Product Attribution Targeting. This can be particularly helpful if you are selling a product that is complementary or that is an accessory to that product.

Let's take iPhones for example. If you have a product that is an iPhone accessory, like a phone case, silicone airpod cover, or dust plug, then you can choose to feature your product next to iPhones or other iPhone accessories.

When you are setting up your targeting for your Amazon ads, make sure to select manual targeting. You are able to really drill down on your target audience through selecting various attributes you would like to target, such as price range, star ratings, product categories, and brands. While Amazon might not collect as much customer information as Facebook, they have gotten pretty good at the ad game, which benefits you, the advertiser.

- Utilize negative keywords

Yes, you still need to implement SEO tactics when you are selling FBA products. But don't worry, there is a very simple explanation as to how to handle keywords and negative keywords.

Let's refer back to out iPhone example. If you are selling silicone covers for Airpods there are certain keywords that you would use. You would want to use keywords like *wireless headphones, iphone, bluetooth,* and *airpods*. You would not want to use words like *android*. Why you ask? Because people that are searching for silicone airpod covers most likely already own an iPhone and already own Airpods or are purchasing the product for someone who does.

Therefore using keywords like *android* in your ads would be a waste of money! So don't do it! Also, leave out keywords that are too general or too short, like *top* or *best*. This is only going to cost you more money in the long run. The point is that you can help to cut your advertising costs by taking advantage of negative keywords.

- Switch up your ad campaign strategies

There are two different kinds of campaigns for Amazon ads - manual and automatic. If you don't know anything about Pay Per Click (PPC) ads, there is a bit of a learning curve with this.

Automated campaigns are pretty much set and forget; however, they aren't always optimal and there is limited control. You should also be checking in on your campaigns periodically to ensure that they are still performing and you aren't wasting money. There is an advantage to using automated campaigns though. They are great for sourcing keywords to then use in your manual campaigns.

If you are new to this whole pay to play thing, then you should take the time to really learn about ads or you can outsource this.

There are many freelancers and agencies available online to assist with your Pay Per Click campaigns that know all about how to optimize your ads so they keep generating sales.

Manual ads are just that, manual. These are something that you really need to keep an eye on. There is a lot that can go into manual campaigns, such as bidding on your keywords. If you don't know what you are doing you can potentially lose a lot of money. While this can sound a little scary, once you have done a few campaigns, then you will quickly become a pro at setting up and maintaining your campaigns.

Your goal with ads is to sell more and spend less. It is suggested that you use various types of Amazon ads and not just stick to one. This can help to optimize your ads, thus generating you more revenue from your ad spend.

CHAPTER SUMMARY

FBA stands for Fulfillment By Amazon. You find a product to sell, ship it to Amazon, and they handle all of the packing, shipping, returns, and customer service. FBA has the advantage of offering their customers Prime shipping.

When you start to generate revenue from your orders, you get paid your cut from Amazon every other week, which creates reliable and consistent income.

You need to keep a few key things in mind when starting your FBA business:

- Make sure you keep your products in stock.
- Consistently turn over your inventory so you don't have to pay Amazon storage fees.
- Advertise and market your FBA business.

As with any business, there are also challenges that are going to arise:

- It costs a bit more to start an FBA business.
- Amazon also requires that you pay service and fulfillment fees.
- If your inventory sits too long you can incur storage fees.
- Prime members that purchase your product might be more likely to return it.
- Amazon can be pretty picky when it comes to certain things.
- Figuring out all the tax stuff can be confusing.

While it might take a bit to get things figured out, there are also many benefits to selling through Amazon FBA:

- You save a ton of time and stress by letting Amazon fulfill your orders.
- Shipping your products from overseas is actually very affordable.
- You don't have to worry about returns and the majority of customer service.
- There is unlimited storage potential.
- Amazon can help to fulfill your orders on other platforms as well.

Choosing a product can be overwhelming; however, if you are confident in your choices and decision then you will go far! FBA is a lot of trial and error, don't get discouraged if your first product isn't a total hit. It is better to go narrower in your niche than to go wider.

FBA often starts with sourcing products from China. This allows for higher profit margins and affordable shipping. Additionally, you can modify a product to make it unique, and you don't have to travel to China to see your products.

It is advised that you establish an LLC when you are selling physical products in the case something happens to a customer and you face legal action.

Generally speaking, people make between a 10-60% profit margin on their products. There are several ways that you can help to drive more traffic to your products:

- Sponsored brands
- Category-specific targeting
- Utilize negative keywords
- Switch up your ad campaign strategies between manual and automatic

CHAPTER RESOURCES
Sourcing products

- Alibaba
- AliExpress

In the next (and last) chapter, we are going to cover everything that you need to know about selling your business for a big payout.

CHAPTER EIGHT
Everything You Need To Know About Selling Your Business For A Big Payout

Now that we have covered the various types of businesses that you can start and run while living your full-time dream RV life, I want to cover selling your business. There can be some major advantages to selling your business, namely a big payout and more freedom! Online businesses can be sold and bought just like traditional brick and mortar businesses.

A good example of someone selling their business for a substantial profit is J.D. Roth from Get Rich Slowly. A personal finance blog that after three years of starting it sold for 7 figures!

While this isn't going to happen with every business, it can really speak to the potential of building an online business, an asset, and selling it for a profit.

In this chapter we are going to cover how and why you should consider building a business with selling it mind. The brokerage process and what metrics you should be tracking in order to get the most out of your sale. We will also cover how long you should keep your business before you consider selling it and the best marketplaces to list your business on when selling it.

WHY YOU SHOULD BUILD A BUSINESS WITH SELLING IN MIND

One of the best things about creating an online business with the intention to sell it is that you can easily rinse and repeat the process. Starting an online business can be done with little to no money and can generate you a huge profit if you are going to sell it. Granted, some types of businesses sell for more than others and others will take more time and money to get started.

If you have started a blog, eCommerce business, publishing business, digital agency, affiliate marketing business, YouTube channel, or even freelancing, there are certain things to keep in mind when preparing to sell your business.

Even if you don't ever plan to sell your business and just implement these tactics, you will be more organized and efficient than most other business owners. You should also take into consideration that your personal circumstances can always change, like traveling full time in your RV. Wouldn't it be great to work on a business for awhile, then be able to sell it and travel around in your RV without having to worry about money?

It is always wise to build your business from the start with the intention to sell, even if you never do. This will help to put systems in place that will keep your business running smoothly with less day to day hands-on operation.

When you are ready to sell a business, potential buyers are going to want to see stats, metrics, and other important information about your business. You should be able to show potential buyers an increased profit over the previous 6-12 months. The longer a business has been profitable, the more it will sell for.

Here are the things you should be keeping track of from the very start:

- Analytics

Make sure that your website is hooked up to Google Analytics! This is especially important if you are selling a blog. Buyers want to know how much traffic that online property is getting and where it is coming from. Being able to show potential buyers your Google Analytics will help solidify your legitimacy as a real business and not that you are inflating your numbers to drive the sale price up. This also helps buyers determine potential areas of growth that they can capitalize on.

As a business owner, having analytics installed and tracking it will help you to determine your ROI. Have you been using Facebook ads to drive traffic to a landing page? Your analytics dashboard will show you if those ads are working (in addition to Facebook's own tools). It's also wise to track your analytics in a separate spreadsheet and note any significant changes. Keep track of what works so you can do more of it.

- Finances

If you haven't already set up a separate account for your business expenses and income, do it now! Not only do you need to be able to show potential buyers expenses and revenue, but you don't want to muddy things up with your personal expenses. You need to be prepared to answer questions about your monthly net revenue, gross margins, and cost of goods sold so that potential buyers can properly assess the value of your business. Overlooking the simplest thing can lose you a sale and a lot of money. If you owe money anywhere the buyer should also be aware of that, so make sure that you are paying your bills on time!

Having your finances in order is also better for you as it will help keep you organized. It is better to be fully aware of your business finances to ensure that you are actually generating revenue from the work you are putting in. You can put together a simple profit and loss statement every month using a simple spreadsheet. There are also many professional software applications for small business owners to help keep your books in order. Freshbooks and Quickbooks are two very popular and easy to use financial platforms. If the thought of bookkeeping makes you cringe, then you can outsource that too! There are many affordable accountants and freelance bookkeepers to help you with keeping your finances in order.

- Standard Operating Procedures

Standard Operating Procedures, otherwise known as SOPs, are like the manual to your business. When you are just starting out with your business it is going to take some time to figure out your processes. Once you have a system down, it's time to create SOPs for everything you do. This can be a very time consuming process, however, it will make a big difference in the sale of your business. The SOP itself is very simple. It is just a detailed document which can include bullet points, photos, screenshots, and videos on a process.

Start with a fairly simple task for your first SOP to get the hang of it. You can ensure that you have created an effective SOP, if you can hand it off to someone else and they can effectively complete the task.

Think about all the different things you do in your business. From email templates to how to properly SEO a post, you should create an SOP for everything you do. That way, when you do sell your business you can hand over your SOPs to the new owner and they will be able to run everything smoothly. SOPs also help your buyer to be able to quickly grow and scale the business rather than just getting themselves another job.

Developing SOPs for yourself can be very beneficial as well, even if you don't intend on selling your business. They are helpful for processes that you do everyday and for ones that you only do once and awhile.

For the processes that you do everyday, SOPs are helpful when you decide to outsource. Your SOP should be put together in a way that you can hand it over to someone who doesn't know your business, and they can effectively complete the task you are asking them to complete.

They are also useful for when you need to do tasks that you don't do very often as they will help to save you time. If you are not doing something everyday you aren't going to be very proficient at it. This is where SOPs are very helpful.

WHEN IS THE RIGHT TIME TO SELL YOUR BUSINESS?

This is the burning question. How long do you have to work on your business before someone is willing to pay you a good chunk of change to buy it from you? The truth is, there is no set time. There are many factors that come into determining the "right" time to sell your business. How much are you trying to make from the sale? Are you selling this business to get an influx of cash for another? What is your goal for the sale?

Before you even think about listing it for sale, you first need to have a good look at your goals and answer those questions. You can, however, get a good estimate as to how much you can sell your business with a simple valuation formula. Take your monthly net profit (your profit minus expenses) from the last six to 12 months and multiply that by a sales multiple of 20 to 60 to get your listing price. For example, a business that has a net profit of about $20,000 a month would list for around $500,000, conservatively. Realistically, it could list for anywhere between $400,000 and $1,200,000.

Notice I said list, not sell for those amounts. This is because there are always negotiations. There have been individuals who have listed their blogs for one amount and bidding wars ensued and the sale price increased to well above the listing price.

When you are considering listing your business you should audit it about six months before it is listed. Now, this does not have to be done professionally, although you could. This simply means taking a good look and fixing any issues with the business that might be unattractive to buyers. Also, during this time, you should be getting your finances, analytics, and SOPs in order for prospective buyers.

If you are working with suppliers, this can add a whole other level of complication. This can be especially important for e-commerce stores. Get your supplier to sign, in writing, that they will continue to honor the same agreement they had with you.

If you are outsourcing any of your business, that should be well documented as well. Sometimes buyers will want to outsource using their own people or they may want to keep freelancers that you are already working with as they should already know the processes.

Generally speaking, people that buy businesses like things to be as automated as possible. So try and find ways to automate and outsource any processes you can. At about three months prior to getting ready to list your business, you should make sure that everything we previously mentioned is all put together. Also make sure to read through all of your SOPs to make sure that they are all up to date and easy to understand. It is wise to get some legal help when drawing up your terms of service.

HOW TO WORK WITH A BROKER TO SELL YOUR BUSINESS

Selling a business is a lot like selling a house, you can either go at it alone or use a broker. When you are selling your business you can sell it on your own. If it is a smaller sale, potentially less than $10,000 this might be a good option. You are, however, in charge of everything when you do a private sale - finding your buyer, data transfers, and negotiations are all left up to you. If you have never made a large sale like this before, this can be rather intimidating. Furthermore, there are a lot of potential downfalls to attempting to sell your business yourself.

Your buyer reach can be drastically limited. So unless you have had people already reaching out to you about buying your business, finding buyers might be an issue. Even if you are able to find buyers, knowing whether or not they are qualified can also be another potential issue. Unfortunately, there are a lot of scammers and tire kickers out there who are going to try and lowball you, especially if they know that you are new at this.

Also, not many people out there are skilled negotiators. You have to consider that the buyer is likely to have more experience buying businesses than you have at selling them, so they might be the one taking over negotiations, and you don't want that! Finally, what about the actual aspect of actually handing everything over? Migrating a business is not a simple task and if issues arise it can become difficult for both the buyer and the seller.

So unless you know how to effectively negotiate and are comfortable migrating everything to a qualified buyer, then you should work with a broker. When you work with a broker they do all the heavy lifting for you. You don't have to worry about what information you gave to what potential buyer; nor do you have to worry about a direct competitor using the vetting process to gain access to all of your information. When you are researching brokers, you should make sure to look for one that is familiar with selling your specific type of business. While there are some similarities in all online businesses, you probably don't want to work with someone that specializes in selling blogs when you run an e-commerce store.

While there are many advantages to working with a broker, such as access to pre-qualified buyers, there are also some downsides.

It can be difficult to find good and experienced brokers as the buying and selling of online businesses is fairly new. Make sure that you are doing your research and ask for references to ensure you are not getting scammed by shady brokers who are only looking to make some money off of you. One good brokerage company to start with, if you are looking to list your business for over $50,000, is Empire Flippers, who charges a 15% commission on the sale. If you are selling a business that is going to generate under $50,000, then Flippa is another great option; they also charge a 15% commission fee.

When you have found a broker that you want to work with, there are several things that you need to put together to get the process started. you will need your traffic data, proof of your revenue and earnings, and proof that you actually own the website, domain, brand, and or trademark. It can take two to four weeks for a broker to analyze your business. After everything is ready to go, you are going to need to set your minimum sale price, this is the lowest price you are willing to go. This also helps to make sure that you aren't wasting your time with buyers who aren't serious.

Even if you decide not to sell your business and just use the tactics discussed here to run your business you will be a much more effective business owner. The more you can automate and systematize, the better.

RINSE AND REPEAT FOR MAXIMUM PROFITS

True entrepreneurs love the process of building something from scratch. When you know how to create an online business you can do it again and again. While some entrepreneurs like to keep all of their businesses and just outsource the major tasks, many also build, sell, and repeat. One thing that entrepreneurs might not be very good at though is being able to determine the fair market value for their business. This, again, is where a broker will come in handy and help you with the process. While building an online business is filled with uncertainty, working with a broker can help you to maximize your efforts and work towards a big payday.

Whether it is building simple websites to sell, e-commerce stores, or blogs, you can always rinse and repeat your process. The thing is that you always learn new things by doing this. Each business is going to be improved from the previous if you are taking each of these businesses as a learning process. You can also learn a lot from the actual sale of a business. Is there something that buyers are looking for that your other business didn't have that would have increased the sale price? If so, apply that to your next business.

WHAT TYPES OF BUSINESSES ARE BROKERS LOOKING FOR

If you have decided that you want to build a business from the ground up with the intention of selling it, here are a few types of businesses that brokers are looking for:

- Individual or packaged AdSense sites
- Sites that use Amazon Associates as the main monetization strategy
- Other affiliate sites
- Dropshipping sites
- e-Commerce stores - Shopify, WooCommerce, etc.
- Software as a Service businesses
- Sites meant to generate leads for other businesses
- Amazon FBA businesses
- Mobile apps
- A productized service, which is where freelancing becomes an actual company

And of course there are certainly sites and businesses that brokers DON'T want. These include:

- Sites and blogs that are not monetized (such as personal and journaling type blogs)
- SEO and link building service sites
- Fan based sites or those that are too similar to social media platforms
- Adult content related sites
- Gambling related sites
- Any site that promotes dubious medical claims or cures
- Anything related to criminal activity, such as hacking

So keep that in mind when you are building your business.

Brokers also look for certain things when it comes to revenue generation. Empire Flippers specifically looks for businesses that are generating at least $500 in net profit per month that is at least six-months old. When you think about it, that is not very difficult to build a business that is generating over $500 a month in net profit in six months. Especially with everything that you have learned in this book!

Once your site is listed with a broker, it's time to sit back and relax while the broker does all the heavy lifting. While some sites and businesses can sell very fast, others might take awhile to find the right buyer. Once the business has officially been sold, the broker handles the transfer of everything with minimal effort from you. While there are no guarantees that your site will sell, a good broker will continue to work with you until the right buyer is found.

In the event that you are selling a smaller site, one that is considered a "starter site," meaning that it doesn't have months or years of traffic and analytics to pull from, you still have options. Flippa is a great platform to sell newer and smaller businesses quick. These can be starter affiliate sites, ecommerce sites, and even domains. Flippa isn't really considered a broker in the traditional sense, but rather an auction site, much like eBay, but for selling businesses.

As Flippa is a marketplace rather than a broker, there are a few key factors to consider. A marketplace lets buyers and sellers communicate directly to one another. Essentially, anyone can post a website for sale and anyone can buy it. Marketplaces that sell businesses generally tend to deal with lower end sales, from $100 to tens of thousands. The great thing about marketplaces as opposed to brokers is they generally get more traffic, which means more potential buyers. This can also mean that there are a lot more people trying to sell their online assets.

If you are in the market to buy a business, a marketplace might be a good place to start. You can skip all the setup and tedious technical tasks associated with setting up a blog or ecommerce site and just buy a starter site. So for a couple hundred to a couple thousand dollars you can have someone else get things started for you.

You can also hire freelancers on sites like Fiverr and UpWork to do this as well if you want to avoid setting things up. The auction setup of a marketplace can also add value to the seller as you are able to drive up a sale price when people are actively bidding on it. When it comes to selling sites on Flippa, higher priced sites often do worse with a lower sales multiple (20x to 60x sales multiple we discussed earlier). But if you are looking for a good quality site at a lower price as a buyer this gives you an advantage.

When you are working with a broker they do they take a commission fee, but they also use things like market research and standardized valuation processes to determine a selling value. Whereas when you list or buy a business off of a marketplace, people generally don't understand sales multipliers and just pick a number that sounds good to them. There is also a lot less red tape when dealing with a marketplace over a broker.

The major disadvantage of selling on Flippa or other marketplaces is the potential to get scammed, lose all your site's info, and all of your money. While no system is perfect, finding a reputable broker will drastically reduce your chances of getting scammed.

CHAPTER SUMMARY

Building a business is so much more than bringing in income, you are building an asset. Once you know what you are doing you can easily rinse and repeat the process of building and selling businesses. You can implement these tactics to become a more effective and efficient business owner.

Potential buyers will want to see:

- Analytics
- An increase in profits over the last 6-12 months
- Finances
- Systems and standard operating procedures

Generally speaking, you should be generating a positive revenue for six to 12 months before selling a business. You can easily come up with a valuation for your business by taking the monthly net profit and applying a sales multiple of 20-60.

Working with a broker can make the whole process a lot smoother and easier.

Types of businesses that sell well:

- Individual or packaged AdSense sites
- Sites that use Amazon Associates as the main monetization strategy
- Other affiliate sites
- Dropshipping sites
- e-Commerce stores - Shopify, WooCommerce, etc.
- Software as a Service businesses
- Sites meant to generate leads for other businesses
- Amazon FBA businesses
- Mobile apps
- A productized service, which is where freelancing becomes an actual company

CHAPTER RESOURCES
Bookkeeping

- Freshbooks
- Quickbooks

Listing your business for sale

- Empire Flippers
- Flippa

FINAL WORDS

WE COVERED A lot in this book, and I realize that it can be overwhelming.

I hope that you realize by now that you don't have to stay stuck in your 9-5 job working for someone else to help them live their dreams. You can work for yourself and have all the freedom that you choose in order to live full-time in your RV on your terms.

Whether or not you already own your dream RV, whether or not you have started a business before or are completely new to these processes, it doesn't matter. You have it in you to achieve your dream life. People are doing it every day, don't get left behind!

It is entirely possible to live your full-time RV life while making a really good income online.

You can make a full-time income with part-time work as a freelancer, blogger, YouTuber, online publisher, affiliate marketer, Amazon FBA, or by selling your business. While it won't necessarily take a lot of money to get started, it is going to take a lot of time and dedication to get going.

- Want to become a freelancer, start looking on the job boards.
- Want to be a blogger, then figure out what you want to blog about and buy a domain and hosting.

- Grab your phone and start recording your first YouTube video.
- Hit that publish button on Amazon and list your first book.
- Start posting those affiliate links.
- Pick a product to sell.
- Then sell your business and rinse and repeat the process again and again!

Now I have given you a lot of information to go out and get started, but it's up to you. You are the only one that is going to make you successful. You can read all the best books, listen to all the best podcasts, watch all the videos, and read all the blogs, but it won't matter unless you are taking action!

Remember, progress is better than perfection. You are going to mess up. You are going to fail, maybe even more than once. You are going to beat your head against the wall a couple of times.

If you want to live your full-time RV life, you have to work for it. No one is going to hand it over to you!

You determine your success. You determine how much work you are willing to put in to achieve your dream. I can't do it for you.

So what are you waiting for?

RESOURCES

Awosika, A. (2019, July 17). Kindle Direct Publishing: How to Make Real Money on Amazon. Retrieved July 21, 2019, from https://smartblogger.com/kindle-publishing/

Barbara. (2019). YouTube Creator Academy: Making advertiser-friendly content [YouTube]. Retrieved July 28, 2019, from https://creatoracademy.youtube.com/page/lesson/advertiser-friendly?cid=earn-money&hl=en

Berger, B. (2017, March 29). 5 Ways to Automate Your Freelance Business. Retrieved July 26, 2019, from https://freelancetofreedom-project.com/5-ways-automate-freelance-business/

Bryant, D. (2014). How to Find the Perfect Product to Import from China and Sell On Amazon | EcomCrew. Retrieved August 2, 2019, from https://www.ecomcrew.com/8-secrets-to-picking-the-perfect-product-to-wholesale-from-china/

Bryant, David. (2018). How to Import from China in 2019 | EcomCrew. Retrieved August 3, 2019, from https://www.ecomcrew.com/how-to-import-from-china/

Carragher, G. (2018, December 13). Chapter 12 How to Leverage the Power of Amazon FBA. Retrieved July 31, 2019, from https://www.bigcommerce.com/blog/amazon-fba/

Carrell, P. (2019, June 25). The Ultimate Guide to The Amazon Associates Program. Retrieved July 31, 2019, from https://www.authorityhacker.com/amazon-associates/

Chesson, D. (2019a, March 15). How To Make An Audiobook: Publishing on ACX and Audiobook Marketing. Retrieved July 23, 2019, from https://kindlepreneur.com/how-to-make-an-audiobook/

Chesson, D. (2019b, July 22). Smashwords vs Draft2Digital vs PublishDrive Review. Retrieved July 23, 2019, from https://kindlepreneur.com/smashwords-vs-draft2digital/

Chesson, D. (2017, December 21). Kindle Select vs KU vs Mass Publication: What's an Author to Do? Retrieved July 23, 2019, from https://kindlepreneur.com/e4-kindle-select-vs-ku-vs-other-markets/

Chesson, D. (2019c, June 27). Book Cover Design Mastery. Retrieved July 22, 2019, from https://kindlepreneur.com/book-cover-design/

Cooke, J. (2013, December 16). Selling Websites Made Easy – How to Sell Your Site With Us - Empire Flippers. Retrieved August 4, 2019, from https://empireflippers.com/how-to-sell-my-website/

Edwards, G. (2018, July 17). Top 10 Affiliate Networks and Programs That Aren't Amazon in 2019 - Empire Flippers. Retrieved July 31, 2019, from https://empireflippers.com/best-affiliate-networks-programs/

Elaine, K. (2019). YouTube Creator Academy: Building Your Audience [YouTube]. Retrieved July 28, 2019, from https://creatoracademy.youtube.com/page/lesson/build-a-sustainable-community?cid=fans

Fiverr. (2019). Fiverr Homepage. Retrieved July 24, 2019, from https://fiverr.com/start-selling

Flynn, P. (2018, October 24). Five Truths About the Mindset of a Successful Entrepreneur. Retrieved July 20, 2019, from https://www.smartpassiveincome.com/mindset-of-a-successful-entrepreneur/

Hogan, C. (2019, March 4). What Is Passive Income and How Do I Build It? Retrieved July 20, 2019, from https://www.daveramsey.com/blog/what-is-passive-income

James, S. (2017, December 14). Are You A Dabbler? Retrieved July 20, 2019, from https://projectlifemastery.com/are-you-a-dabbler/

Kniep, S. (2017, October 9). The mindset you MUST have if you want to build passive income | Just One Dime Blog. Retrieved July 20, 2019, from https://justonedime.com/blog/the-mindset-you-must-have-if-you-want-to-build-your-passive-income

Masters, J. (2019, May 24). Selling a Blog for 7 Figures after 3 years of Starting it with JD Roth - Eventual Millionaire. Retrieved August 5, 2019, from https://eventualmillionaire.com/jd-roth/

Mijatovic, B. (2017, November 2). How to Prepare and Sell Your Online Business - Empire Flippers. Retrieved August 4, 2019, from https://empireflippers.com/prepare-sell-online-business/

Miller, L. (2018, May 23). 7 Myths About Passive Income You Can't Afford to Believe. Retrieved August 4, 2019, from https://www.entrepreneur.com/article/313137

Morrow, J. (2019, June 7). How to Make Money Blogging (Free Guide for 2019). Retrieved July 27, 2019, from https://smartblogger.com/make-money-blogging/

Muller, B. (2019, July 12). SEO 101: Why is it important? – Beginner's Guide to SEO. Retrieved July 27, 2019, from https://moz.com/beginners-guide-to-seo/why-search-engine-marketing-is-necessary

Patel, N. (2019, February 15). Affiliate Marketing Made Simple: A Step-by-Step Guide. Retrieved July 30, 2019, from https://neilpatel.com/what-is-affiliate-marketing/

Perkins, G. (2018, July 31). How to Start a Youtube Channel: Step-by-Step for Beginners [YouTube]. Retrieved July 27, 2019, from https://www.youtube.com/watch?v=AE6M3hcHnyw

Perez, S. (2018, June 22). YouTube introduces channel memberships, merchandise and premieres. Retrieved July 28, 2019, from https://techcrunch.com/2018/06/21/youtube-introduces-channel-memberships-merchandise-and-premieres/

Ramirez, V. (2018, February 11). Guide: How I Made $7,645 Part-time On UpWork in Less than 2 Months. Retrieved July 24, 2019, from https://www.isvictorious.com/upwork-freelancing-guide/

Sameera. (2019). YouTube Creator Academy: Ads on YouTube [YouTube]. Retrieved July 28, 2019, from https://creatoracademy.youtube.com/page/lesson/ad-types?cid=earn-money

Sell My Site. (2018, June 13). Ultimate Guide to Buying & Selling on Flippa. Retrieved August 4, 2019, from https://sellmysite.com/buy-sell-flippa/

Skrba, A. (2018, April 8). What is a Blog? - Explanation of Terms Blog, Blogging & Blogger (2019). Retrieved July 26, 2019, from https://firstsiteguide.com/what-is-blog/

Stephen. (2019). YouTube Creator Academy: Make Money on YouTube [YouTube]. Retrieved July 28, 2019, from https://creatoracademy.youtube.com/page/lesson/revenue-basics

Swinunski, M. (2019, March 25). Build, Grow, Sell, and Repeat. - Empire Flippers. Retrieved August 4, 2019, from https://empire-flippers.com/build-grow-sell-and-repeat/

Valentine, M. (2018, May 4). How to Start a Successful YouTube Channel in this Day and Age | Goalcast. Retrieved July 27, 2019, from https://www.goalcast.com/2018/03/06/how-to-start-a-youtube-channel/

Wordstream. (2019, May 1). 8 Advanced Tips for Advertising on Amazon. Retrieved August 5, 2019, from https://www.wordstream.com/blog/ws/2019/05/01/amazon-advertising-tips

THE RV
LIFESTYLE
MANUAL

Living as a Boondocking Expert
How to Swap Your Day Job for Travel
and Adventure on the Open Road

JEREMY FROST

Life is either a daring adventure or nothing at all.
– **Helen Keller**

INTRODUCTION

IMAGINE VISITING A peaceful town one day, eating the local cuisine and checking out the sights, and then traveling past scenic views and gorgeous vistas the next.

A lot of people might say, "Aren't you talking about a backpacker lifestyle?"

Hardly. I am talking about the RV lifestyle.

If the backpacker lifestyle is like Tony Stark before he created the Iron Man suit, then the RV lifestyle is like Tony with the nanosuit he used in the final *Avengers* movie; you are surrounded by awesome tech, you have abundant comfort and amenities, and you can travel better than a backpacker.

If you haven't watched *The Avengers* or any of the Marvel movies and failed to get the above reference, then let's try looking at it this way:

Would you enjoy walking with a backpack strapped to your body as you hitchhike your way around the country, trying to replenish your cash reserves while thinking of where you might find a decent place to sleep? Or would you prefer to move around in a comfortable land vehicle that looks like a studio apartment on wheels?

The RV lifestyle is the answer to the nine-to-five grind. It is the wake-up call that you have been waiting for, letting you know that if you are indeed planning on spending most of your time in an enclosed space (a.k.a. your office), then you might as well do it in one that keeps moving from one place to another (a.k.a. in an RV). You are meant to experience the world, but that might not happen if you take the elevator (or, for the unlucky ones, the stairs) to the same place every single day. And if you are among those wondering how you are going to break free from this monotonous lifestyle, an RV is your answer.

Of course, after answering the 'what,' where you figured out what you are supposed to do to change the course of your life, you are then stuck with another important question.

How?

How are you going to get into an RV and move around without enough resources? How are you going to procure food, fuel, and other basic necessities? How can you continue to earn a stable income while you are on the road?

All your answers are going to be provided by this book. You are going to learn about the fundamentals behind downsizing from a house or a condo to an RV. Once you reduce the space you are living in to the interior of your mobile home, then you are going to learn how to travel full-time (never thought you would hear the words, "travel full-time," did you?).

We are even going to examine what kind of RV you should purchase. This is to ensure you are not looking at an RV and probably thinking of getting a loan, selling everything you have, and making a deal with the devil just to get it. You are going to be guided through what supplies you might need to pack into the RV and where you could stay while you are traveling. This book is not just aiming to be informative; it is aiming to be the instruction manual to your RV lifestyle.

But why me? Of all the people in the world, what makes me an RV expert?

It is because I have lived the RV lifestyle. Actually, let me rephrase that. I have been a part of the RV lifestyle since I was young.

My parents were avid campers. They loved the outdoors and living life with the simple joy of experiencing what this world can offer us. Imagine this: you are surrounded by the stillness of nature, or the sounds of nature's inhabitants. There is the unmistakable smell of freshness that you cannot easily find in a city. All around you are spectacular views that you thought you would never see in your lifetime.

Whenever it was time to go RVing, my parents and I wouldn't just spend a few hours or a few days outside; we would be out there for several months! And that's how I grew familiar with the lifestyle, understanding all there is to know about how to live in an RV, what to do when you are moving around, and how to become part of the lifestyle. In fact, my dad used to use his RV to drive me to my daily baseball games. A single activity that used to only take place over several months eventually became a significant part of my life.

Fast forward to the present. I have now spent over five years traveling around the world in motorhomes, campers, and vans. I know one thing about this life, and that is that it is quite fleeting. I had to ask myself if it was worth spending my days simply dredging through the mundanity of life, or if I could do something more to live better. With that being said, I hope this book gives you the motivation to get into your RV and hit the road, if you haven't already done so.

Once you have read this book, you are going to have the tools to become part of an adventure. You are going to discover how you can embrace freedom and travel, without being attached to the corporate rat race.

Think about it.

You now have no schedule. There is no compulsion to attend a meeting and explain your tasks for the day, or the targets you had missed by a minute margin. You won't have to indulge in office politics just so you can have a better standing with the boss man or woman. There is no need to be competitive with anyone.

Your life is in your hands, and you are going to drive it (both literally and metaphorically).

And guess what? You are not the first person who I have helped embrace this lifestyle. I've worked with hundreds of people who are in the same position you are in right now. They knew that they wanted to take destiny by the reins (or in this case, the steering wheel), and make a difference in their lives. I have helped them make that difference.

And now, it is your turn.

You don't have to be an expert on RVs or camping. All you need to do is have that mindset of wanting to make a difference in your life. When you have confirmed that you indeed do want to make this change, then don't think about making it 'someday.' The truth about the 'someday' statement is that, usually, those things don't happen, or if they do, they occur in a manner you might not be satisfied with.

So get ready to enter a journey, as each chapter in this book will take you that much closer to your goal.

Get ready to swap your day job for travel and adventure on the open road.

Let's rev this journey!

CHAPTER 1
You Have Way Too Much Stuff!

YOU MIGHT HAVE a lot of possessions with you right now. Just look around and you'll find a visual confirmation of that statement.

When you are about to make the shift to living full-time in an RV, you are going to have to make some important decisions. Mostly, you are going to make the not-so-easy choice of figuring out just what you would like to have in your RV. If you quickly assess all the things you have in your home, you are likely going to feel that there are many things that are important to you. But importance does not mean you can take them with you—you can't fit your entire shoe wardrobe into your RV. You are going to have to make some choices.

At this point, you might be thinking about how difficult it is going to be, parting with some of your possessions. You might even wonder if there are others out there who are about to go through the same dilemma you are going to face. Isn't the world heading towards the ownership of more materialistic things, rather than walking away from them?

Do you want to know the reality of the situation? People are actually giving up on materialistic possessions in exchange for experiences. In fact, it has been estimated that over 78% of millennials—who have an astonishing $1.3 trillion purchasing power—are choosing to spend that hard-earned money on experiences rather than objects (Power, 2018).

The point is that more and more people are less afraid to give up on things in exchange for something more valuable: the chance to live through something intangible and wonderful. However, the problem they face is not knowing how to keep on living the life they choose. They find themselves saving up some money, traveling to a country and experiencing new things, then returning back to their day jobs. Rinse and repeat. They are not able to keep the traveling lifestyle sustainable.

Nevertheless, what we are going to do is not merely travel someplace and return back to our daily grind. We are going to keep on traveling for as long as our hearts desire.

With that idea in mind, it becomes less difficult to get rid of some of the things currently taking up space in your home.

DOWNSIZING FOR THE COUNT

Let's get down to the nitty-gritty details of the downsizing process. Remember that it does not matter if you are living in a beachfront property or a small studio. Downsizing is a tough job, unless you have been living a minimalist lifestyle, in which case, you might find the task of preparing your RV considerably easier.

To clearly explain the concept of downsizing, I have broken down the process into simple steps.

A Downsizing Plan

Your plan brings together various factors to help keep the downsizing process running smoothly. To develop an effective downsizing plan, think of the below points or questions while keeping in mind the space in the RV you are moving into (which we will discuss in the next chapter):

- What items from your home can you get rid of?
- What can you absolutely not get rid of?
- How can you donate, sell, or throw away items that you won't need?
- Which items will you donate, sell, or throw away?

Items You Cannot Get Rid Of

This is a difficult junction in the downsizing process, mostly because of the fact that if we ask ourselves what we would like to get rid of, we might just answer by saying, "Absolutely nothing!"

But in order to find out what you should keep, think of the following points or questions:

- Are there any items that have sentimental value to you?
- Think of those items that you have spent a lot of money on and loathe to part with it.
- Write a list of the items you have held onto for a long time.
- Do you have objects or items you haven't used yet, but think they hold potential for the future?

Once you have made a list of the items you cannot get rid of, try giving a reason as to why you cannot let go of them.

This is an important step because, oftentimes, we are unsure of the actual reason why we would like to hold on to some things. That pocket watch your father gave you when you were young is something you should always hold on to. But the $300 shoes you bought thinking they would impress your friends won't really matter for your RV life. When you start evaluating your arsenal of items with logic and rational thought, then you can actually begin to understand what you should include in your RV and what you can get rid of.

Downsize Your Clothes

Now that you have a pile of clothes you cannot get rid of, look through those items again and pick the pieces you will need while you are RVing. In order to make it a little bit easier on you, here is a list of necessary items:

- Casual t-shirts and shorts
- A few button-up shirts
- A couple formal wear (or dress) options
- Jeans
- Slacks and track shirts/pants (if you have them)
- Windbreaker and fleece jacket
- Raincoat
- A pair of casual shoes and a pair of formal shoes/shoes that go with formal wear (essentially, nothing that looks appropriate for jogging)
- Hiking boots, or boots for cold weather
- Bathrobe
- Night clothes
- Slippers
- Sandals
- Bathroom slippers
- Sunglasses
- Wraparound glasses with wind protection

- A few face masks (for those who have certain allergies or for any other reason that might come up)
- Umbrellas (one should be enough, but you could keep a couple if you have space)

Donate or Sell Your Clothes

While you are downsizing your wardrobe, think about the items that you could donate to a local charity or other non-profit organizations. At this point, you might feel like you have many clothes you would not like to part with, but the key is to think of downsizing in a logical manner. For example, if you have a dozen dresses, pick one or two you really like and keep the rest for donation or sale. It's the same with everything else. If you have a shoe closet with about 200 different pairs of shoes, you won't be needing all of them on your trip. Make a rational decision and let the rest go to someone in need.

Trash Your Clothes

If you have clothes that are faded, have stains or tears, or might be damaged beyond repair, throw them away. Some people might decide to donate such clothes, but I like to believe that if you don't like wearing them, don't give them to someone else. If you are giving something away, make sure it is in relatively good condition. It's a matter of principle similar to the idea that if you wouldn't eat something, don't give the food to someone else.

Store Some Clothes

You might come across certain clothes that have a sentimental value. Don't bring them in your RV. Rather, store them in your home for safekeeping. If there are any other items of clothing you simply must store, then make sure you do it now.

Essential Kitchen Items to Take

You know what they say—if you don't prepare, then you'd better beware.

Actually, nobody said that, but you can't deny that it is true. When you plan ahead, then you are not leaving anything to chance. You're making the right moves and choices to ensure that you have greater control over as many future scenarios as possible. While it is true that the future is uncertain and we cannot always prepare for every outcome, it goes without saying that you should expect the best and prepare for the worst. And yes, somebody actually said that.

Your next course of action is to take all the items you will require in your mobile kitchen. Here is a handy list you can use as a template:

- Dinner plates, coffee mugs, cereal bowls, dessert dishes
- Drinking and wine glasses
- Chef's knife
- Spoons (both tablespoons and teaspoons), forks, and dinner knives
- Whisk
- Grater
- Cutting board
- Can opener
- Measuring cups and measuring spoons
- Colander
- Mixing bowls
- Vegetable peeler

- Potato masher
- Tongs
- Corkscrew or wine bottle opener
- Stainless steel skillet
- Saucepans (one small, one medium, and one large)
- Baking sheet pan
- Casserole dish
- Cookie sheet
- Storage containers
- Aluminum foil
- Plastic wrap
- Oven mittens
- Immersion blender
- Plastic tablecloth
- Table mats, dish cloths, and napkins
- Clips to close bags
- Heavy sponge
- Dishwashing liquid
- Small trash bags
- Coffee pot (get a percolator one on the off chance you don't have a sufficient power source)
- Small grill
- BBQ utensils
- Small toaster

Kitchen Items to Donate or Sell

Here are points to consider when you are donating or selling kitchen items:

- Items that are duplicates.

- Things that you might not need for an RV, like cheese spreaders, salad spinners, and garlic presses.
- Other items you do not use often.

Kitchen Items to Trash

Just like your clothing, throw away any kitchen item that is broken, damaged, or rusted.

Essential Bedding/Sofa Items to Take

Time to add a bit of comfort in your RV. For the most part, choosing the items you would like to take for bedding (or sofa, if your RV has one) is fairly simple. Nevertheless, here is a handy list for inspiration:

- Pillows and a few pillowcases
- At least one change of bed linens
- Comforter
- Blankets
- A few cushions
- Your favorite soft toy, if you have one (hey, no judgment passed—it's your RV!)

Bedding Items to Donate or Sell

- Items that are too bulky or are not required for an RV, such as large cushions, bed linens that are too big, curtains, and anything of the like.
- Any duplicates, ranging from your pillowcases to bedspreads.

Bedding Items to Store

If you have certain items with sentimental value, keep them with you. Plan everything carefully so you don't accidentally give away or sell something that might later prove to be valuable to you or to someone else.

Documents to Keep in the RV

There are those documents you would like to always have with you, just in case a situation occurs where you might need to show them as proof of something or to complete a process. Below is a list that should help you get started, but feel free to add anything you think is absolutely invaluable.

- Passports, birth certificates, marriage documents, and documents that prove the purchase of the RV.
- Multiple copies of all the above documents.
- Any insurance you may need.
- Multiple copies of all the above documents.
- Multiple passport-size photographs.
- Identification cards, credit cards, insurance cards (if you have them), social security cards (if you have them), and other forms or cards or special identifications. Also, make sure you have multiple copies of these documents as well.
- If you have important records, such as tax records, consider scanning them all and storing them electronically. Since records might be useful, however, you can keep them with you in the RV as well.

Documents to Donate or Sell

I'm just kidding. I would never ask you to donate or sell any documents! And for that matter, let's assume you are not supposed to send any documents to the trash. However, we do need to add one additional section here that is going to be quite useful.

Documents to Store Electronically

It is going to be difficult getting rid of those framed photographs of your family, but rather than put all of them together into boxes, simply upload them into a cloud space or an online storage platform.

Additionally, make sure that as many documents as possible under the "Documents to Keep in the RV" section are stored electronically, both to save on space and make them easier to locate if and when you need them.

Office Supplies to Keep in Your RV

Make sure you bring your laptop or computer and all the cables and devices that go along with it. One of the most efficient ways to store all these cables is by putting them in Ziplock bags, where each bag is used for one cable. If you need an additional cable for certain types (such as an HDMI), then you can put both in the same Ziplock.

If you have space, bring your printer or scanner as well, but it is not necessary to do so. When short on space, store any other additional electronic devices in your home.

Keep a ream of A4-sized paper with you, along with a couple of the below items (except in the case of paper clips and safety pins, where you can keep a small box of them):

- Pens and pencils
- Erasers
- Pencil sharpeners
- Notepads
- Tape
- Permanent markers and highlighters (just choose one or two colors)
- Staplers
- Paper clips
- Safety pins

Office Items to Put into Storage

Do not take too many pens or office supplies with you. It might be nice to have 200 different kinds of pens, but you won't be needing all of them on your travels. Pare down to the necessities and store the rest away.

Tools for Your RV

On your journey, it might be useful to have a few tools with you to deal with any emergency situations. I have created a handy list for you below—but note that you don't have to have every single tool from the list. If space is a concern, at least make sure you bring the essential ones.

Essential Items

- Assorted tools such as hammers, wrenches, screwdrivers, and pliers
- Assorted nails, screws, and bolts
- One small bucket
- Drill and bits

- One extension cord (if you have space, add in another one)
- Water filter for the RV
- Flashlights
- Batteries
- Hoses (you can get different- colored ones, where one is used for regular water and the other for drinking water)
- Jumper cables
- Rubber gloves for cleaning and emptying tanks
- Soap and a brush for washing the vehicle
- Zip ties
- WD40

Non-essential Items

- Ax
- Bungee cords (might also become useful if you are into extreme sports)
- Work gloves and coveralls (not entirely necessary, but add it if you have them around in your home)
- Flare kit
- Measuring tape
- Brake transmission fluid, power steering fluid, and motor oil (you can also get these at a nearby gas station)
- Shovel

Tools You Should Store

Put all the stuff like paint, electronic tools, and other hardware, into storage. Make sure you are absolutely strict about storing such tools because a lot of them will require significant space if you try to bring them into your RV.

Additional Items

If you have the space for it, you can also add in a couple of outdoor folding chairs, a grill, a small folding table, and an outdoor mat.

You can also attach a step ladder to the back of the RV. This is useful when you need to do cleaning and maintenance activities on the top of your vehicle.

Take road maps, guides, and other useful navigational books and documents with you. Of course, you can always find everything you need on your phone—as long as you have an Internet connection.

The key phrase in the above statement is "as long as you have an Internet connection." Sometimes, you might need assistance when you have low connectivity or no service whatsoever.

Selling Your House After Moving Into an RV

Once again, I'm only joking. Please don't sell your house! There are a few ways you can earn income through your house while you travel, but more on that later. For now, let us look at just one more section.

Hobbies You Can Bring to Your RV

Obviously, you cannot pack all your possible hobbies into your RV. Some of them, like gardening, are things you just won't be able to do, especially with the equipment that is required. However, there are certain activities you can include in your RV (and maybe even adopt as a new hobby).

- If you are into painting, you can pack in an easel and some paints if you have the space for it.

- Books can be digitized, so you might want to subscribe to Amazon or Kobo books to get all your reading material.
- Stitching, crocheting, and wood carving can also be made portable.
- Pack a single guitar if you can, but otherwise most musical instruments won't fit into the RV. If you can find instruments that are the size of the guitar or smaller and you can find the extra space, bring them along.

EVALUATING FUTURE PURCHASES

In this section, make a list of the things you might purchase in the future. You will likely need to brainstorm a little bit, but making this list will help you greatly during your travels.

- You will tend to avoid any clutter in the future. When you plan ahead, you know the space you have in your RV and your purchases will be made accordingly.
- With proper planning, you can think long and hard about the things you want. Sometimes, you might feel like some items need to be added to your already growing pile of things, but upon careful evaluation, you might find alternatives.
- When you make a list of the things you would like to purchase, you might automatically start checking to see if you still have some of the essential items with you. If, as you go through the list, you notice your supply of staples is getting low, make a quick purchase (if you would like to replenish staples).
- Keep everything organized in its own space so that it is easy to check for inventory, which will also help you get an idea of what space you might have for future purchases.

- Whenever you add something to your purchase list, think of the dimensions and weight of the object you are adding. This will allow you to plan your RV space much more efficiently.

So, you see, with the right planning, you can make the most use of your space. But what's the point of all that downsizing if you don't even have an RV? After all, that is going to be your first decision: the choice of mobile home you would like to invest in.

For that reason, I shall let my esteemed and knowledgeable colleague, Sir Chapter 2, take over.

CHAPTER 2
Choosing the Right RV for You

R**IGHT NOW, I'M** sure you are excited to jump into the details of the various types of RVs you can invest in. That's really good; you need to have that excitement. However, there are a few factors that you have to think about before you even consider buying an RV.

POINTS TO REMEMBER BEFORE BUYING AN RV

Buying an RV is not as simple as getting a new car (which is also not a simple decision). There are some essential criteria you need to think about. Some people think that considering the below points dashes their hopes of ever owning an RV, but I beg to differ. I think you have to be realistic when you are buying an RV. In fact, this point goes for any big investment you make throughout your life.

Think about it, how long did it take you to decide to buy your home or move into an apartment? You must have checked out the location, price, amenities, accessibility to transportation, internet access, building materials, age of the building, neighborhood, and probably a dozen other factors before you decided to buy, rent, or lease the place.

Let us look at some of the requirements you should consider before you decide to buy your RV.

Point #1: Type of Camping

Think about the type of camping that you would like to do. For the purpose of this book, we are going to assume that you will be in your RV full-time.

However, if you would like to focus on primitive camping, you could think about investing in a travel trailer or a pop-up tent.

For our purpose, however, we are going to be looking at Class As, Class Cs, airstreams, or maybe even vintages—but more on that later in this chapter.

Point #2: Your Journey

It is important to have a rough idea of the places you would like to travel to. By knowing this, you can understand what kind of RV you would like to get. For example, if you are thinking of staying at public parks, then you should ideally consider getting an RV that is no more than 32 feet. With smaller units, you won't encounter many problems.

If you are thinking of investing in bigger RVs, then you should also think about the stops you are going to make on your journey. Where are some of the ideal places you can do with an RV of the size that you are going to get?

The important thing to remember about this point is that you don't have to get into the details of the journey; that's for another chapter. You are simply developing a rough idea to help you make an appropriate purchase decision.

Point #3: Stay for Long or Travel Constantly?

The bigger the RV, the more fuel it consumes. This could become an important factor in deciding what kind of RV you would like for longer travels. Furthermore, it is not just about the size, but all the features packed into the vehicle. More electrical components means more fuel for your journey.

On the flipside, if you are planning to stay in one spot for a longer duration, then you should think about what your vehicle can offer you in terms of everyday living requirements.

When you are traveling, you might also want to consider the terrain you may traverse. If you are planning to ride off the beaten track, consider the overall build of the RV. Most vehicles are built low to the ground, which means navigating through uneven terrain may pose as a challenge for your RV. Remember that RV maintenance may be expensive, so damaging it frequently is really going to put a dent in your wallet.

Point #4: RV Occupants

How many people are going to travel in the RV? Are you going to be bringing any pets? If so, will they need to go outside frequently, or are they just indoor pets? Are kids going to join you in the RV? Do you need a small space for them to play or study?

The above questions will help you choose an RV that offers sufficient space to provide for all your answers. For example, if you have a camper van, then you are not going to be able to fit two dogs and your family, as well.

Point #5: Your Budget

This is probably something you will be taking into account a lot. To be honest, not many people like thinking about the budget, but it is important to take note of your finances. More importantly, you need to have a realistic projection of your purchase. Let's say you are planning to spend just under $50,000 for an RV because that is all you will require. That's great! Perhaps you are going to be traveling alone and don't need all the extra baggage or people. But then again, after considering all the previous options, you may think of investing in a bigger RV, yet realize you can easily shell out $150,000 (key word here is 'easily') for a well-appointed vehicle. You should not be in a position where you are borrowing money from different sources for your RV. If you are, there is a separate section below for you that you need to take a look at. You might also need to consider the possibility of a fifth wheel and a truck, but more on that in Point #7.

Point #6: Getting Money

I don't recommend this option. The reason why you are shifting to a mobile home is not just to downsize in reality, but in your life as well. You are minimizing the influence of materialistic objects, living your life to the fullest, and avoiding the stress of bills and debts. If you start borrowing money from the bank or other financial institutions, then your debts will follow you wherever you go. No open space will eliminate the presence of impending loans from your mind.

For your peace of mind, try not to borrow money.

However, an RV is an expensive investment, so I can understand the need to consider financing options. For that reason, here are a few tips to consider:

- Make sure you calculate your loan amount and the monthly payment scheme. When you are calculating this, you need to make it as realistic as possible. Do not try and give yourself wiggle room. This is your future and finances we are talking about, after all.
- When calculating the debt payment scheme, make sure you include all the expenses you might require while using your RV. Do you have enough for the loans you have taken? Can you comfortably pay off what you've borrowed?
- Do not borrow any amount you cannot pay back within two years. I don't recommend working on your loan for more than two years because of the stress it could bring to your life. Think about this way, do you really want to spend more than the first couple of years of your RV life worrying about loans?
- Keep a strict budget during the payment period. Do not overspend when you are living in the RV. Make sure that you prioritize your basic needs first (including fuel for the RV and other such expenses), then focus on your debts, and finally on anything else that you require.
- I've said this before and I am going to repeat it again: expect the best and prepare for the worst. What happens during a medical emergency? What about urgent repairs to your RV? Are you able to pay for such expenses and still pay back your debts?
- Would you need to invest in a fifth wheel and a truck? If so, are you able to meet those investments and pay off your debts, as well?

As you can see, borrowing money is a pretty tough choice. Make sure you are absolutely certain of your decision. If you think your mind is rather biased towards the idea of a loan because you are tempted to get a fancy RV, then seek advice from your friends, family, or experts in your area. Get a second and third opinion before you think about borrowing any money.

Point #7: Truck

If you are planning to get yourself a travel trailer, then you might need a truck or a fifth wheel.

So, what exactly is this 'fifth wheel' we are talking about? It sounds like four wheels are going on a double date, and Mr. Fifth Wheel is all by himself.

That's not the kind of fifth wheel we are talking about, and quite frankly, I think the term 'third wheel' is used for anybody, regardless of how many people they are with.

But I digress; back to the point I am trying to make. A fifth wheel is a coupling mechanism that is used to attach the truck to the trailer.

The above point might be a little confusing, so let me break it down for you.

There are two types of travel trailers: those that are attached to the back bumper of a truck, or any other form of towing vehicle, and those attached to the bed of the towing vehicle. A ball-and-coupler hitch mechanism is typically used to attach the trailer to the towing vehicle. A fifth-wheel trailer, on the other hand, is not attached to your rear bumper. Rather, it is connected to the bed of a truck or the towing vehicle using a special jaw hitch. As you can see, if you are getting a travel trailer, then you should ideally have a truck that is big enough to pull it. If you are planning on getting a fifth-wheel trailer, you might need to invest in the fifth wheel mechanism.

Think about this when you are considering your RV choices.

Point #8: The Driver

This might sound like an odd point to make note of, but trust me when I say that it might be useful in the long run. If you have people traveling with you and would like to share the driving responsibilities with someone else, then you need to get an RV that is convenient for both you and the other person to drive.

If you need to check out how it feels like to be in the RV of your choosing, you can try taking one out for a test run. This will give you a sense of what you are buying, or if you would like to consider a different purchase.

Point #9: Features

You should ideally think about the features if you have sufficient funds to pay for them, as the more features an RV has, the more expensive it might get. Different RVs provide different features. The best way to choose something that is right for you is to consider your lifestyle. Think of some of the luxuries you used to enjoy and see if you can afford them when it comes to your RV.

Here are a few options you might think about:

- Television
- Bunk bed
- Dining table
- Washer and dryer
- Multipurpose areas
- A desk
- Basement storage
- Two bathrooms

Once you have considered the above, and all the other points in this list, then you are able to make an informed decision about your RV.

But while we are on the subject of important points to think about, it is time we dispel some myths that have cropped up around RVs and RV lifestyles.

IMPORTANT MYTHS TO DEBUNK

Myth #1: RVs are Cheap

While you can find inexpensive options and perhaps even get a second-hand vehicle at a highly discounted rate, there is no such thing as a cheap RV.

Once you purchase your RV, there are additional maintenance, upkeep, and repair costs you have to think about. At one point in time, you could find RV parks that cost about $5 a night. These days, though, you are going to come across those that easily hit the $40 per night mark. Make sure you are not under the false impression that RVing is going to be cheap simply because you did not get an expensive vehicle.

Myth #2: RV Costs Are Similar to Regular Vehicle Costs

When you are taking your RV for maintenance (or doing it yourself), it is not as easy as just popping open the hood and check to see if the brake fluid is looking good. The entire machinery of an RV is complex. The air conditioning system itself is much bigger than what you would find in a regular vehicle.

You are traveling with a portable home. There are going to be more costs involved than a simple four-wheel drive or sedan.

Even simply cleaning an RV is going to cost more since you have a bigger mode of transport (much bigger, to be honest) than a car. Think about this when you are purchasing your RV.

Myth #3: RVs Have a Lot of Storage Space

You are going to realize just how untrue this is when you actually enter an RV. This is the main reason why I have a separate chapter on downsizing, because I want people to be prepared before they step into an RV.

You cannot take anything and everything when you are in an RV. Sure, the bigger the RV, the more space you get to play around with, but that does not necessarily mean you should stuff in as many things as possible.

Myth #4: You Don't Have to Consider Safety During Purchase

This is wrong. Make sure you ask the dealer about the quality of the RV. In fact, make sure you are purchasing your RV from a trusted dealer. Or, in the case of a second-hand RV, make sure you are checking it for quality.

One of the things to consider is road vibration. As you are traveling, things get bounced around, including the entire frame of the RV. By making sure your purchase is made out of good materials, you can ensure its longevity. Don't skimp on your investment just to end up with a low-quality RV because of its price point.

Myth #5: I Made This Myth List to Scare You into Not Buying an RV

Absolutely not true. I truly want you to be part of this incredible life and wonderful journey I make with my own RV. But most of all, I want you to make an informed decision after considering all the facts and realities. I don't want you jumping to conclusions and regretting your investment later. Take your time to run through every factor before making the purchase of your RV. In fact, I recommend thinking things through even before you decide to downsize your home. And if you are already aware of all the points and myths, it doesn't hurt to think about them again.

Now, after you have thought about the points and myths, it is time to move on to the RV itself.

TYPES OF RVS

As you look around, you'll find different kinds of RVs available on the market based on size, features, and affordability. Here are their typical classifications:

Class-A: Motorhomes

Think about the mobile home bus of Will Smith, and you will then have a pretty good idea of what a Class-A RV looks like.

These RVs are the biggest things in the world and come with all the features that make it seem like you are traveling in a moving apartment. You typically do not find many second-hand or used Class-As on the road. That is simply because of the significant investment that goes into these RVs. You can find flat-screen TVs, ottomans, multiple sofas, large floor space, and a plethora of other features.

For Class-A trailers, here are some of the manufacturers you can look into:

- Newmar Corporation
- Tiffin Motorhomes

- Entegra Coach
- American Coach

Class-C: Motorhome

No, I have not made a mistake in the arrangement of the classes. Class-C is indeed much better than the Bs.

You can easily spot Class-Cs because they are typically built on the chassis of a van. In fact, one of their most notable features is the fact that their roof extends over the cab of the vehicle. Additionally, unless they have been repainted by the owners, they usually come in muted colors like grey, beige, dull white, and other similar shades.

These are cheaper than Class-As, and while they don't have all the technological marvels of Class-As, they do have an excellent balance of space and features for first time travelers.

For Class-C trailers, here are some of the manufacturers you can look into:

- Lazy Daze
- Winnebago Industries
- Dynamax
- Entegra Coach

Class-B: Motorhomes and Campervans

This entire class has a wide variety of options, all falling under the umbrella term of 'campervan.'

You can find large vans that have toilets and showers, or you could opt for the smaller vans with pop tops that look like they should be camped in at Woodstock. When you are looking at the bigger Class-Cs, you have RVs with enough space for one person to move from the front to the back of the van, with beds, stovetops, sinks, refrigerators, and other features to cater to your basic needs. But what they lack in space, they make up with one major advantage: they do not need a towing vehicle to move them around. They can also easily stop at many gas stations, unlike other forms of RVs.

For Class-B trailers, here are some of the manufacturers you can look into:

- Coach House
- Leisure Travel Vans
- Pleasure-Way Industries

School Buses

Seriously, school bus RVs are actually a thing!

There are many people who have opted to convert a school bus to a motorhome. The advantage is you can transform the interior in a manner that suits your preference. On the flipside, you have to either do all the work yourself, or pay someone to fix up the RV for you. You will also have to invest in all the materials needed for the RV.

Travel Trailers

The basic idea behind any travel trailer is that you attach a large living space to your truck or towing vehicle. They are usually compact, but you do have the option of making them larger. These are attached to the bumper of your towing vehicle. They also come in a few other options, which we are going to look at in the next few sections.

For your travel trailer requirements, here are some of the manufacturers you can look into:

- Outdoors RV
- Northwood Manufacturing
- Oliver Travel Trailers

Travel Trailers: Fifth Wheels

We've already discussed what fifth-wheel trailers are all about—they hook up to the bed of your truck. Fifth-wheel trailers can come in various sizes; they can be as large as Class-A motorhomes or they can be smaller than Class-Cs. It is all up to you. But do note that the bigger the trailer, the bigger (and more powerful) the towing vehicle you will need to pull it along.

For fifth-wheel trailers, here are some of the manufacturers you can look into:

- Outdoors RV
- New Horizons RV
- Northwood Manufacturing
- Grand Design RV

Travel Trailers: Teardrops

If you put Class-As on one end of the trailer spectrum, then teardrops fall on the other end. These regular-vehicle-sized trailers are the smallest option you can find. Some are made to include just a bedding space and are used primarily by people who want to have greater options when they are parking their vehicles. They are also easier to tow than other models of trailers.

For teardrop trailers, here are some of the manufacturers you can look into:

- nüCamp
- Little Guy Trailers

Travel Trailers: Pop Ups

What makes these trailers unique is that they can expand using tent sections and other kinds of 'pop ups.' These expansions are usually done to create more space for bedrooms and other facilities. Pop ups can have simple mechanisms, like tents, that give more room space and canopies that add shade outside the trailer. Or, they can have sections of the trailer that actually extend outwards to make more space. Not many people prefer to use pop ups, though, because of all the extra maintenance that goes into these and the fact that these RVs can be rather cumbersome for those who are planning to live in them. They are ideal for camping or short-term trips.

For pop up trailers, here are some of the manufacturers you can look into:

- Jayco
- Flagstaff
- LivinLite

Travel Trailers: Airstreams

These kinds of travel trailers are fairly easy to spot, as well. They usually have an aluminum body that is sometimes rounded. What they lack in space, they make up for in their build. They are solid and highly durable mobile homes. While they are usually smaller than regular sized fifth-wheels, they provide sturdiness that is not usually found in other trailers.

Airstreams are not just a type of trailer, but they are a brand, as well. Simply check out Airstream USA to see their range of travel trailers.

FLOOR PLANS TO THINK ABOUT

Here is the simple truth about floorplans: you can get one to fit any need, budget, or requirement. So don't worry if you feel like you are not going to get something that fits your tastes. When you are looking for the floor plan, there are three essential factors to consider.

Bed Space

If you are going to invest in a larger RV, you might not have a problem with bed space. However, if you do not have a lot of room, you will have to think about how you are going to fit in the bed. Many RVers find that placing the bed all the way in the back of the RV provides enough space in between for other amenities. But bedding ideas are entirely up to you.

Even if you are planning to get a spacious RV, think about the bed arrangement and how conveniently it can be accessed.

Bathroom Access

Where is the bathroom going to be? Is it going to be close to the bed? If that is the case, do you have enough space for a toilet and a shower? Would you like to add a sliding door or hinged door?

Think about the above questions as you plan out the bathroom space. When you are looking at different options of RVs, think about how these considerations can guide your purchasing decisions.

Refrigerator

If your RV comes with a refrigerator, then see if you are happy with where it is positioned or if you wish to make changes to it. In those cases where there is no refrigerator, you might have to go about installing one yourself. Measure the space where you are going to place your refrigerator to get a clear idea of the size of the refrigerator you will need. Look for any alternatives. Think about movement and proximity to other objects and doors.

Closet Space

Sometimes, having slides tend to block out access to the closets. In fact, you could even have a refrigerator whose doors could block you from reaching to other things. Some people are okay with such minor inconveniences and learn to live in their RVs around these obstructions. If you think certain temporary blockages are workable, then you might have a certain degree of flexibility in choosing an RV. However, if you feel you need everything to be in its own space without preventing access to other areas of the RV, then you might have to think more carefully about how you are going to arrange things in your RV.

Work Space

Since you might be working from your RV, it may be a good idea to have a designated work space for yourself. Some people are comfortable spending a little extra to add in a work space, but if you are short on budget, consider turning one of the other spaces into a work space.

Alternatively, you can bring some foldable chairs and a table that you can set up outside your RV.

Dining Space

Some people are not picky about the dining space—they can turn any seated surface into a place to eat. However, if you have certain preferences, then make sure you are creating a space that fits well with your RV's floor plan. In Class-Cs and Class-Bs, you might end up making compromises with the space.

Space Jam!

In quite a few scenarios, you might not be able to get all the features crammed into your RV. If you do, then you may have a hard time accessing some of them. The space in your RV is going to be truly cramped, even closed off. The best way to decide how you would like to use the space is by listing the features that you want in your RV and that occupy the floor space. For example, let us assume that you have created the list below.

- Dining space
- Bathroom
- Refrigerator
- Work space
- Sofa area
- Recliner
- Fireplace
- Wardrobe

Your next step is to arrange them in the order of importance. Don't worry about adding features for aesthetic purposes right now—think of utility and usefulness. Let us now assume that after putting much thought into it, you have narrowed down the list to the below.

- Bathroom
- Refrigerator
- Dining space
- Work space
- Sofa area
- Wardrobe
- Fireplace
- Recliner

Start arranging the above features into your RV's space in the order of their appearance on the list. For example, you first measure the bathroom space and make sure that it is as close to your expectations as possible. Then, move on to the refrigerator and see if it fits well into your RV. Next, see if you have enough room for the dining space. If there is a special work space, that is an added bonus. At this point, you will have a clear idea of what you can do with the remaining floor space. Let's assume you have no space for a sofa, but can you add a small recliner instead? If not, perhaps an easy chair?

In such a manner, you can discover if there is enough space for the rest of the features on the list. Through efficient planning, you can have an RV that contains all your important needs within it, and if you do find some extra space, go right ahead and pack it with the additions you like!

LEARNING TO DRIVE YOUR RV

You might be wondering to yourself, why would I need to learn to drive a vehicle when I have been driving for X number of years?

The truth is that driving an RV is unlike operating any other vehicle you might have driven before. For that reason, here are a few simple tips you need to keep in mind before getting behind the steering wheel of your RV.

Tip #1: Start With the PMI

PMI stands for Preventative Maintenance Inspections. Check your tires, brakes, turn signals, the bulbs inside the RV, and other features so that you do not receive a nasty surprise while on the road. Make sure you have clean linens on the bed and clean surfaces before you start out.

Check your inventory to see if you need to replenish anything, but most importantly, focus on the RV itself. You need to make sure everything is hazard-free before you move out.

Tip #2: Understand Turning Radius

When you turn, the radius taken by an RV is considerably greater than those taken by smaller vehicles. It is a good idea to identify the turn radius and keep it in mind before driving. Too often, people miscalculate because they suddenly realize they have been thinking about their four-wheel drive back at home, rather than their RV, which happens because of the long-time use of that familiar vehicle.

Tip #3: Practice on Empty Roads

Before you begin your adventure, make sure you have practiced driving your RV on empty roads. Check and see how easy it is to make turns. Get a feel for your RV so you can easily get yourself out of a jam when you encounter one.

Tip #4: Secure the Stuff in Your Motorhome

You do not want your cutlery flying around every time you make a turn in your RV. The best way to avoid that is by making sure you secure everything in your RV. If you need to use special locks or tags for that purpose, then do so before you head out.

Oh, and don't use your mobile phone while driving. Make sure that is secured somewhere, too, where it won't be a distraction to you while you're operating the vehicle.

Tip #5: Secure the Stuff Outside Your Motorhome

If you have objects attached to the outside of your motorhome, ensure that you have them tied down. You do not want that ladder attached to the back of your RV flying off and landing on top of the roof of someone else's car, making that person wonder if it has started raining stepladders all of a sudden.

For your own safety, and for the safety of others, make sure everything that could detach from the RV is fastened securely to the vehicle.

Tip #6: Maintain More Braking Distance

You are not racing anywhere, so make sure you maintain a safe braking distance from the vehicle in front of you. Ideally, you should be able to apply brakes well in advance, or at least give yourself the opportunity to slow down to a stop. Remember that your RV is probably packing more power than the vehicle in front of you.

Tip #7: Drive Slower

As I said, you are not racing anywhere. Drive slowly. Don't worry about people honking at you to go faster. Prudence is always the preferable option.

Think about it this way. If you are driving along a rather slippery road, then you need to have more control of your RV. The RV is a big machine, so if it loses traction on the road because you are driving too fast, then you are going to have an incredibly difficult time getting it back under control. Eventually, you will be involved in a fatal accident.

Instead, just keep calm and drive slowly.

Tip #8: Plan Your Route in Advance

Nothing ever goes perfectly. That is probably one of life's biggest principles. However, that does not mean you should leave everything to chance. Make sure you have a route planned out. That way, even if you have to divert, you have an idea of where to go back to.

Tip #9: Do Not Allow People to Walk Around While the RV is Moving

Encourage people to sit or lie down as much as possible. If anyone needs to use the facilities, let them know they should be doing so when you are on a relatively straight road and your speed is within a comfortable range.

This is another reason why you should drive slowly. If someone wants to use the bathroom while you are driving and you are going too fast and lose control of your RV, the bathroom is going to be a death trap for the people still inside.

Tip #10: Keep Your RV's Height in Mind

Certain underpasses and areas might have height limits. Make sure you know the height of your vehicle so you can navigate through them or, if you have to, around them using another access point.

Tip #11: Take Turns Slowly

Drive slow. Take turns slower.

There is no need to rush. Keep the turn radius in your mind when you are navigating turns. Remember your RV's height, as well, because as you turn, the center of gravity shifts. Your RV can tilt slightly and you might need to adjust the speed accordingly.

With all of the tips and recommendations in this chapter, you are ready for the RV lifestyle. Or are you? Perhaps you might have to consider a few more things before you shift to your motorhome.

CHAPTER 3
Transitioning into the RV Lifestyle

ONE DOES NOT simply pack everything and decide to shift to an RV lifestyle. You have to take a few things about your new mobile life into consideration.

There are certain mental, emotional, and logistical aspects to living in an RV. For example, if you are an introvert, how do you handle life on the road? What about a person who might experience claustrophobia when stuck in an enclosed space for too long? What happens if you are a social butterfly and would like to meet people on your journey?

Some people might think these questions above are rather trivial, but you need to understand them in order to have a sense of emotional and mental stability.

The first thing we are going to do in this chapter is discover how to have a fulfilling life within the RV lifestyle.

ADJUSTING TO YOUR NEW LIFE ON THE ROAD

There are a few things you need to remember before you start your journey, as well as certain factors to consider during your journey.

Think About Your Life Before Living It

It does not matter if you are planning to travel alone, with your pets, with friends, or with your family. Having a plan in mind helps you understand what you might need to do with certain components of the RV life. Here are a few questions for you to think about. You can add as many questions to the list below as you would like to get a full picture of your plan.

- What are you going to do with your residence once you have moved out? Are you planning to keep it locked, or would you like to entrust it to someone else?
- Do you have a way to earn income while on the road (more on this in a later chapter to help give you ideas of income sources while you are on the road)?
- How are you going to stay connected?
- Are you comfortable living on backcountry areas and campgrounds, or are you only looking to stay in 5-star RV resorts?

Work Out a Rough Budget

You need to be aware of what kind of expenses you are going to have while you're traveling. In Chapter 1, we discovered how to establish a rudimentary budgeting system. Here, it's time to add in as many details as you would like so that you are completely aware of all the expenses you are going to incur on your journey.

You can also take this time to create your expected budget. This will help you understand just how much you are going to spend on a monthly basis, overall. You can then fix a number that will be your monthly limit. Having such a limit will prevent you from accidentally overspending.

Living the Lifestyle

You are transitioning from one lifestyle to the next. This means you are still going to have to perform your daily chores, run errands, pay bills, and engage in your usual activities. For this reason, you need to ask yourself if you are the kind of person who prefers to stay in a particular location for a while, or if you would like to constantly move from one place to another. Are you comfortable boondocking out in the national forests, or are you only interested in using campgrounds?

By knowing your travel style, you might gain a better idea of how you are going to take care of your daily tasks and find time for your work and other projects.

HOW TO SURVIVE LIVING IN A SMALL SPACE!

Once you have decided to live in an RV, it is not just about taking care of your daily needs, but also about making the most out of a tiny space. How can one do it? What should one remember when living in such a small area?

Multi-Purpose Spaces

Since you are not going to have a lot of space for everything, you should think about how you are going to use existing surfaces for various purposes. For example, your dining table could serve as your work space and for preparing your meals.

You might also have to put many items in one spot. Often, you might find that your laptop and work tech will be sharing space with your groceries and other random items. Be prepared for this, and even try to think about ways you can create spaces that can be used for many purposes.

Make Time for the Outdoors

Living in a small space means you are not going to get a lot of natural light. Even if you have windows, you might not receive the required amount of natural light to maintain your health. Take time to step outside and enjoy the outdoors. This could also be the perfect time to pick up some healthy habits, such as walking or jogging. Whatever it may be, it will allow you to explore the world outside, get some fresh air, and even flex your muscles.

Besides, you might need to stretch our legs once in a while, so why not do it through an activity?

Learn to Cook Simple Meals

Sometimes, you won't have the opportunity to prepare a fancy five-course meal, especially when you are driving for long hours. This is why it's a good idea to try and learn quick one-pot meals. There are so many options available online to offer you variety and they don't take too much time to prepare.

However, this does not mean you can never prepare a nice dinner or a wonderful breakfast, but it is better to know how to cook different kinds of meals so you are prepared for any occasion. For example, let's say you are running out of supplies and you still have a day to go before you can restock. By knowing how to cook a nice and simple meal, you can make use of what you have to the fullest.

Meet People

If you are a person who enjoys social interaction, then get to know people when you park your RV at campgrounds or other places, if you have the opportunity. Also, do not lose touch with the people who matter in your life back at home. Contact your friends and family as frequently as you can so you do not feel a sense of loneliness as you travel the road.

Get a Pet

Pets are a great addition to the RV, if you have the space for them. Make sure your pet can easily fit within the vehicle, and that they are comfortable and fed properly. During my journeys, I have come across quite an interesting collection of pets, including a goat, owl, pig, gecko, and even a parrot. Of course, most of these people were either traveling alone or in pairs. Some had their families with them, but they were efficient in the way they managed their RVs and pets.

Pets are truly wonderful companions. Make sure you have your RV prepared for them and, more importantly, make sure they are RV-ready. For example, you cannot think about getting huskies in your RV. These dogs are hyperactive and require a lot of activity during the day. Know your RV before you get your pet.

The Dirty Stuff

Sometimes, you are going to be carrying dirt from the outdoors into your RV. Make sure you have a system in place to deal with that. For example, you can put a mat outside and ask people to remove their shoes before they enter the vehicle. Or, you can sweep the RV twice a day to ensure that people do not spread the dirt everywhere. Ideally, I think it would be better if you try and ensure that your RV is a no-footwear zone (except perhaps near the entrance).

Cables

It is always useful to have extension cords so you can charge your devices, however, this could lead to wire clutter. Make sure you are putting away your chargers and other wires when you are done using them. This not only allows others to use the extension cords, but also keeps your RV tidy.

Have a Comfortable Routine

An RV is a small space. This means you are going to create noise and interruptions, even when you do not want to. This might become obvious when you have others traveling with you. If you notice others sleeping or resting, then try to minimize your noise as much as possible. In fact, try to establish a routine where everyone can get some quiet time if they need it.

Clean Up

Try to establish frequent cleaning routines. When your space looks clean, it sometimes does not matter if it is small or big. Make sure you have healthy habits, such as cleaning up after you eat, keeping everything tidy and the floors swept, and maintaining the RV itself so it looks clean on the outside. Of course, cleaning an RV is a much longer process, so you don't have to do this every day. But keep a routine so you don't forget to give your motorhome some cleaning every so often.

Keep Things Organized

Have a spot for everything you own. Do not throw things in random places. Organizing helps you in two ways:

- It keeps the interior of the RV neat and tidy.
- You are able to find things when you need them. You might think things won't get misplaced in such a small space, but

they can, and you could end up spending some time trying to recover them.

Keep Bedding Simple

This might sound like a rather odd point to make, but when you add too many items on your bed, it tends to make the space look smaller. Use plain colors and avoid placing too many cushions and objects on the bed. This way, the space appears considerably bigger.

Perform Regular Maintenance

Your RV comes with a water system and probably an air conditioning system. Since it might be pretty expensive to take care of things in the long run, make sure you are maintaining them as much as possible.

To do this, try to learn more about your RV. You can ask for help from the RV dealership, from local RVers, or you could find plenty of useful information online. No matter what your problem is, chances are there is a solution in the world of the internet.

TRAVELING WITH KIDS AND ANIMALS

To better deal with this section, let's split them into two. We are going to first focus on RVing with your kids, and then move on to pets.

Tips for RVing With Your Kids

Get the Right RV

This is probably self-explanatory, but make sure your RV is appropriate for your kids. Typically, when you are getting your RV, you will be told how many people the RV is ideal for. Some RVs are good for three to four people, while others give a wider option with two to seven people. Knowing this will help you decide which motorhome will give you as much comfort as possible during your travels.

Plan the Trip in Advance

It is fun to be spontaneous, and while you can still do that, it is always better to have a rough plan for your travels. This allows you to determine specific stops for taking a break, having food, using the facilities, restocking certain items, or simply allowing the kids to experience the outdoors for a bit.

Even if you would prefer not to have a plan, make sure you have a map or guide with the locations of important places. These could include gas stations, campgrounds, parks, and other areas for your RV. This way, even if you need to make an emergency stop for any reason, you can quickly refer to your map and find the closest campground or RV spot for your motorhome.

You can even get some incredible RV apps to help you plan your journey or guide you towards the nearest essential spot.

Check out some of these apps:

- InRoute Route Planner
- Roadtrippers
- Google Trips

I would also recommend the following navigation app:

- CoPilot RV: I like this app since you can actually use it offline! The best part is you can enter in your RV's height and width, and it will calculate the best route to reach a specific location without running into low bridges and tight tunnels—definitely something that might be useful when you don't have the best internet connection.

These apps give you added benefits or make your trip more interesting:

- Gas Buddy: If you don't just want to know where the nearest gas station is, but where the cheapest one is, then you need this app.
- TuneIn Radio: You get to tune in to local radio stations for news or your favorite sport updates.

For finding spots for camping, you can use the below apps:

- Reserve America
- Recreation.gov
- iOverlander
- Campendium

Stay Updated

Try to keep yourself informed about the latest news and information for the areas you are in. This helps you find out weather updates and other details that could be useful for your travels—for example, finding out there is construction coming up on one of the highways you have been traveling on could give you the idea to try an alternative route. The same goes for the weather and local news. Here are some options you can look into:

- TuneIn Radio
- NPR One
- Pandora

Pack Lightly

One mistake most people make is that they try to cram as many clothes and other objects into their suitcases as possible. But you won't be needing all those clothes, and they only end up taking valuable space you could have used for something else.

Make sure you travel light. Remember the list we made in the chapter on downsizing? Stick to that. Also, make sure you use soft luggage as it will not only help prevent any injuries (as with hard luggage), but you might also be able to squeeze them together more efficiently in tight spaces. Hard luggage tends to take up more space, and there is nothing you can do to make them occupy a smaller space.

Ban the Electronics

Make the trip all about the trip.

Removing electronic devices allows you to connect with your kids and gives you the opportunity to experience the journey with them without any distractions. Additionally, you are going to save a lot of electricity in the RV (and eventually fuel costs) by minimizing electronics as much as possible.

Keep Portable Snacks

Sometimes, you might need to travel for a fair amount of time before you reach a particular camp. Additionally, you may not be able to make multiple emergency stops every time your kids might get hungry as you might disrupt traffic, or there may not be any place to park your RV.

To deal with such scenarios, make sure you pack snacks in portable containers. By doing so, you won't have to worry about making emergency stops to eat a quick bite.

Don't Drive Every Day

Even if you are planning to travel consistently, make sure you plan stops for a few days at a time. This allows you to unwind and perform important chores in the RV, while also giving the kids a chance to head outside. Small breaks such as these allow you to relax both physically and mentally.

You don't have to be in a hurry to get anywhere. The main purpose of having an RV lifestyle is to attain a sense of fulfillment. That might not happen if you are constantly moving around without a break.

BBQ Nights and S'mores

Make your RV trip fun. Have BBQ nights and enjoy some s'mores by the fire. Play fun games with your kids. Take them out trekking on adventures. You'll not only bond well with your children, but they'll have a lot of fun while on the trip!

I mean, thinking about the next stop and planning camping is all well and good, but what's the point if you are not having fun?!

Try to Avoid Extreme Temperatures

This is where the need to stay informed comes in. While you might have the immune system of the Incredible Hulk, the same cannot be said about your children, so try to avoid places with extreme temperatures or temperature fluctuations.

Or, in other words, stay updated!

TIPS FOR RVING WITH PETS
Rules of the Road

While it might seem rather natural to allow your pets to roam around the RV while you are driving, it could actually be dangerous for both you and the pet (and the RV, of course).

While you might be following the speed limits, the same cannot be said about other drivers. You will need to keep your eyes on the road to deal with any troublesome motorists. But even if you are on an empty stretch of road, wandering pets tend to cause distractions, which is something you shouldn't have to worry about when driving.

Pack the Essentials

When in doubt, make a list.

Get all the essentials for your pet. Here is a list I made to give you a little guidance on what you should include, but feel free to modify it as you see fit:

- Leash
- Crates
- Litter
- Toys
- Pet carriers
- Refuse bags for pet droppings
- Brush and grooming items

I know, a lot of people might frown upon the idea of putting their pets in carriers, but think about what matters most: a temporary safe enclosure for your pet, or a potential accident waiting to happen?

Update Your Pet IDs and Bring Them With You

As with the list you made during the downsizing process, make sure you get the actual IDs of your pets. Make a few copies and also save them virtually.

Add Exercise as Your Daily Habit

Moving around your muscles and body from time to time is not just healthy for you, but your pet as well. As we discussed in the section about RVing with your kids, try not to drive every day. Stop for a while at camps and take your pet out for walks. If your pet is a bird, you might want to keep it outdoors for a while. Of course, you might also want to keep it on a leash if you are worried that your bird might fly away.

Get a Pet Bathing Kit

Many people often overlook this part and end up giving their pet baths using the bathroom or the water hose (which is not the ideal way to clean your pet). Make space for a bathing kit for your pet so you are not wondering where the nearest pool with clear water is.

MAKING YOUR RV FEEL LIKE HOME

Home is where the heart is, even if said home is moving around a lot.

People often wonder if they can make their RV feel a little more like the home they've left behind. It is definitely possible, and I am going to show you how.

Home Tip #1: Change the RV Mattress

The mattress that comes with your RV might not be suitable for you, so make sure you change it to something a bit more comfortable. If you feel that getting a brand-new mattress is not something you would like to invest in, there are cheaper alternatives. For one, you can get a mattress topper, which is essentially a layer of bedding you add on top of your mattress. Alternatively, you could even take the mattress from your home and put it in your RV if the mattress can fit on the RV's bed.

Home Tip #2: Add Wall Decor

Include pictures, stickers, or other wall decorations to bring a little color and life to your RV. Adding wall clocks showing times from different parts of the world is also a wonderful addition.

Here are some other ideas you can consider:

- A map of the country or region
- Photo frames containing fun sayings or messages
- Hanging pots and plants (make sure they are completely secure, or you could choose artificial plants, as well). HINT: You can choose to take down the pots and plants when you are traveling and set them up again after you have parked your RV, but that means you have to manage your space very well since these decorative items can take up a lot of space.
- LED lights
- Flameless candles (they set the ambience without setting your RV on fire)
- Hanging wicker baskets is a great idea for décor and storage

Home Tip #3: Use Oil Diffuser

Get your RV smelling fresh. It doesn't take too long for the RV to accumulate a plethora of scents from your travels. Using an oil diffuser can make all the difference in the world. Scents such as eucalyptus add a little freshness into the air, while rose can provide a wonderful sweet smell. Look at different oils and find the one that suits you. If you are traveling with other people, let them smell the scents before you buy them so you can find out if anyone is allergic to the fragrance.

Home Tip #4: Home Comforts

Remember how we talked about bringing bathroom slippers and cutlery? Many people prefer to buy new items for the RV, but I like to have things from my home because they make the RV feel lived in. Bring in your favorite coffee mug. Get your comfortable home slippers. Add your welcome mats, if you would like. Things you have already used before entering your RV have a sense of value to them, and bringing them to your RV transfers that value to your motorhome.

Home Tip #5: Add Curtains

If your RV comes with valences, then see if you can replace them with curtains. With such a simple addition, the interior of your RV transforms into something comfortable and cozy.

Home Tip #6: Bring Your Favorite Tunes

I am serious. Playing your favorite music in the RV can actually make a whole lot of difference.

Let me give you an example.

If you had a particular playlist you used to play while working from home, then playing that playlist in your RV can actually make you feel like you are once again working from home.

But there are other situations where music could very well be the remedy. You are going to face some challenges while RVing—perhaps it could begin to rain heavily and you might have to stop for a while until the weather changes for the better. You are unable to do anything but sit and wait out the downpour. During those times, think about the moments when you used to play your favorite songs at home, the ones you or your entire family would enjoy. Perhaps you and your family used to take turns playing music because one person could not decide whose music was better until, eventually, everyone decided they should each have a turn at picking a track.

Recreate the same experience in your RV. Either put on a nice playlist or let people take turns playing some of their favorite songs.

Allow for this experience to happen not just during a chaotic situation, but for other times as well. Enjoy your favorite music and the preferred music of your passengers whenever they are in the mood, just like you would at home.

Home Tip #7: The Great Outdoors

Just because you have an RV does not mean you cannot extend your home space to the great outdoors. In fact, that is one of the benefits of having such a vehicle. You can have so many unique outdoor vistas, locations, and sights to experience.

To do this, see if you have enough space to pack an outdoor tent. In fact, if you are staying at a particular spot for a few days, you can even use the tent as an extension of your living space. Toss in a mat and a few cushions and you could work, relax, or just have fun outside.

Home Tip #8: Keep Things Neat and Organized

I've already made a point about this, but it requires mentioning again because this time, it concerns the environment you are trying to maintain. Clutter not only disrupts the homey atmosphere you are trying to establish, but also has an impact on your mind. More clutter makes your space feel untidy and creates a sense of chaos, subconsciously creating a sense of chaos in your mind as well.

Have you ever been in the middle of a traffic jam and felt the stress it gives you? Now think back to those times you were in the presence of nature, where there were not a lot of people around and you felt peaceful and serene.

The same situation applies here. When you are in the presence of cutter and chaos, your mind reacts to it accordingly. If there is a sense of order and tidiness, however, your mind itself begins to project order and tidiness into your life.

With the above tips, you have made a wonderful transition to your RV lifestyle, but transitioning is only the first step. Now you have to start living in your RV and take care of it. For that, we move on to Chapter 4.

CHAPTER 4
What You Need to Know Before You Go!

THE PREPARATIONS ARE complete. The plans have been set. You are certain that you have looked into everything. The time has come for you to begin your journey.

But as you are journeying in your RV, there are a few things you need to keep in mind, especially when it comes to the maintenance of your motorhome.

HOW DO YOU DUMP THE TANKS?

Cleaning the RV holding tanks is not a job anyone would willingly take. However, it has to be done and you have to dispose of the human waste in a proper manner (while taking care to not disturb the environment).

There are some simple steps to take care of the tanks, but before we start doing that, let's see what we might need in order to prepare ourselves.

Prepping With the Right Tools

You will need the following tools before you start dumping anything out of your RV:

- Disposable gloves
- Rinse hose to flush out the black water
- Bleach wipes for sanitation
- Clear sewer adaptor
- Sewer extension hose (ideally 30 feet long)
- Hose elbow
- Hand sanitizer to clean your hands after you are done

Types of RV Tanks

Depending on how your RV has been set up, you might find the below tanks attached to your motorhome:

- Black tank to take care of the wastewater and sewage from your toilet
- Grey tank to deal with the water from your shower and sinks
- Freshwater tank that stores clean water (this is the water you use in the shower and sinks)

We are going to start by learning how to empty the black water tank first.

Waste Disposal

Ideally, look for RV dump stations and other designated areas for taking care of the black water tank. These areas and installations are specially-made to provide you with the convenience of cleaning out your tanks in a safe, sanitary manner. Once you have located these tanks, follow the process below:

1. Put on your gloves and make sure there are no tears in the fabric. Make sure the valves of the grey and black tanks are closed before you move on to the next step.

2. Now start by attaching one end of the hose to the sewer or dump station hole. You can also make use of a hose elbow and a hose ring to connect the hose properly to the dump station or sewer hole. By doing so, you can attach the hose securely. However, this is not always needed if you are careful when getting rid of the waste. Also, don't just leave your hose lying around when you are draining your RV. Make sure you are either holding it or securing it using the elbow and hose ring. Even with additional measures to secure the hose, it is still prudent to hold the hose in case there is an unexpected disaster and you need to react quickly.
3. Connect the other end of the hose to the black water tank. You might think people are careful when it comes to attaching their hoses, but you would be surprised by how many people do not double check to make sure everything has been fastened. One way to connect the hose to the tank is by first positioning the opening underneath the black tank outlet. Once done, open the flap and allow any drips to fall directly into the hose. When you notice the drips have stopped entirely, connect the hose to the tank and secure it properly.
4. When you are confident that everything is properly attached, open the black tank water valve first. You will hear the noise of wastage rushing through the hose. Eventually, you will start to hear a trickling sound.
5. Do not remove the hose yet. Flush the black tank with water to clean it completely. Certain RVs have the ability to use the clean water from the grey water tank to perform this task. If not, you might have a different setup to help you with this process. Typically, you might also have a rinse system in the

RV that you can connect to the black tank. Fill the tank up to two-thirds with water and then flush out the tank once again. This will allow you to clean the tank, as well as the hose.
6. Make sure you close the valve to your black water tank.
7. When you are done, remove the end of the hose that is connected to the tank first. Lift it up so you can drain any leftover materials from the pipe straight down into the dump station or sewer hole. If you have a separate hose for cleaning, use that to clean the hose instead.
8. Finally, detach the end of the hose connected to the dump station or sewer hole.
9. Repeat steps 2 through 8 for the grey water tank.

The Dumping of the Dump Stations

One of the things people have begun to notice is that RV dump stations are slowly disappearing. This is because people are not careful when they are cleaning out their RVs; they simply don't care about spillage, or they misuse the facilities.

When you are using a dump station, make sure you are following proper etiquette.

- The dump stations are only meant for the contents of your holding tank. Don't throw anything else in there.
- If you accidentally make a mess or spill something, be respectful and courteous—clean up after yourself!
- Do not dump garbage or trash in the area. Find designated spots to discard any other form of waste materials.
- Do not discard your gloves or any other equipment into the sewer hole.

- Most dump stations or sewer holes come with a flap or covering. Make sure you close them. You don't have to leave it open for the next person.
- Don't use the dump stations to simply park your RV while you begin to clean other materials and objects. Leave it open for the next traveler to use.

Cleaning the Tanks

You have successfully emptied the tanks. But what about the tanks themselves? How can you make sure they are clean?

Here are a few ways to take care of your tank.

Once you have dumped your tanks, you can then use tank treatments (one such example is the RV Digest-It). All you have to do is pour it down your toilet. It removes any foul smell and also helps in digesting the waste quickly. It is recommended that you use treatment products frequently, as this helps in avoiding any clogs or waste build-up in the tank.

There are also items called cleaning wands that help you clean out the tank more effectively. Connect them to any garden hose and you can then use them to dislodge any waste materials from your RV tank.

Arranging the Waste Equipment

Make sure any items that are used for waste disposal are kept separately from other items in your RV. You might also need to clean these materials.

Make sure you strap on your rubber gloves and use a cleaning solvent or solution for the purpose.

You can also sanitize the items by taking a large bucket and filling it with water. Add in a solution of bleach (usually at the rate of ¼ cup for every gallon of water). Soak the items inside the solution for at least four hours. You don't have to do this frequently—if you can perform this just once a month, you are good to go. You can also do this before the start of each season.

Additional Help

One of the apps I think you might find invaluable is the Sanidumps RV Dump Station Locator. This app allows you to find the closest dump station. All the results you look for are located on Google Maps, allowing you to easily find navigable routes towards that particular dump station. A lot of people might not think of how useful this app is until they are left searching for the nearest dump station.

REGULAR MAINTENANCE ON THE ROAD

Just like your tank, your RV is going to need some maintenance as well. To a lot of people, this might seem like an overwhelming task since they are often left wondering what part of the RV they should start working on first.

Here is a list to get you started.

Maintenance #1: Look at the Seams and Seals of the RV

Use your ladder (or some other way) to inspect the roof of your RV. Check for any leakages that could let rainwater into the interior of the vehicle. Check the skylights, vents, edges, and air conditioning unit. If you notice any leaks, you can make use of any number of sealants available in the market. However, try to choose a sealant that works well with the material your RV is made of. Think about getting the gaps or holes fixed sometime in the near future to provide a more long-term solution to the problem.

Maintenance #2: Check Your Tire Pressure and Wheel Nuts

Your RV's tires are going to suffer quite a bit of abuse (not to mention with the weight of the RV on them). Make sure you are checking the air pressure in your wheels to maintain safety on the road. Look at the lug nuts to see if any of them have come loose, even just a little, and make sure the tires are not overinflated. This could cause them to explode, leading to some serious accidents on the road. The seasons affect the tire pressure, as well. For example, if you are planning to spend time in a particular location during winter, make sure you check your tires before heading out because tire pressure can drop significantly during this time of year.

Maintenance #3: Check the Batteries

Your aim with the batteries is to keep them fully charged, but people don't always pay attention to that as it means making frequent trips to the garage. However, what you can do is make sure the batteries are in good condition before your long trips.

Maintenance #4: Maintain Your RV's Tanks

We had already seen a step-by-step process of how you can maintain the tanks of your RV. Do not leave your RV tanks uncleaned or undrained for a long time. There are numerous products that can help you with tank treatment. Here are some products that have received some good reviews:

- Happy Campers Organic RV Holding Tank Treatment

- Rid-X RV Toilet Treatment Liquid
- Walex TOI-91799 Porta-Pak Holding Tank Deodorizer

These are just some of the products on the market you can make use of. Whether you would like to remove odor or dislodge waste materials, there is a product out there for you.

Maintenance #5: Keep Your RV's Brakes Maintained

Check out the wheel bearings and other brake parts to ensure they are well lubricated. Brake repairs can be rather expensive, so frequent maintenance can help you avoid shelling out hundreds of dollars for a replacement.

Maintenance #6: Check Your RV's Slide-Outs

If your RV comes with many parts that can slide out, then make sure you check them regularly, especially their seams and seals. If you notice dust or other particles, clean them out so you don't have any obstructions causing further damage.

Maintenance #7: Replace the Fuel, Coolant, Air, and Hydraulic Filters in Your RV

The first thing you have to do before you even think about replacing anything is to check the current condition of the parts. Look at the fuel, coolant, air, and hydraulic filters to see if they need a bit of cleaning. Do not take any chances if you see them ruined beyond repair.

Maintenance #8: Towing Vehicle Connection

Some people establish an electrical connection between the towing vehicle and the trailer. If you do, make sure this connection is working properly without a hitch. This connection is useful for various reasons. One of them is the fact that when you hit the brakes, the brake lights on the trailer will light up. The same goes for the signal indicator as well.

WHY YOUR RV NEEDS TO BE LEVEL

Often, people don't think about leveling their RV, but this is an important part of taking care of your motorhome. It doesn't matter if you are looking to camp somewhere temporarily or if you are planning to use the RV as a new home, leveling helps you make the most of some of the RV's features.

If you don't level your RV, you might experience one (or all) of the below problems.

Warm Refrigerator

You wake up one morning to the smell of freshness in the air. A nice breakfast would be perfect. So you head out to the refrigerator to get your ingredients. However, as soon as you open the door, you notice the food has spoiled. What's more, the beer is warm as coffee (the horror!).

What just happened? The refrigerator was working perfectly yesterday. In fact, you can still taste the lingering flavor of the nice, chilled beer you were enjoying just last night.

Time for a bit of science. Liquid ammonia flows through a part of the evaporator coils inside the refrigerator, which are usually at low temperatures. But one of the key components to keep this process going is gravity. As you probably already know, liquids don't go uphill (if it does, then you have discovered something magnificent). If your RV is uneven, one side of the refrigerator is tilted upwards, preventing the liquid from reaching that place. The ammonia can actually pool and settle, causing a blockage in your refrigerator. If you continue to operate your refrigerator at an uneven level, especially for a prolonged period of time, you may be hit with an expensive repair bill (which, when combined with a warm beer, is a recipe for a bad mood).

You can use a spirit level to check for any tilts. You might already know about these handy tools. They usually have a liquid inside them that is often green in color. There is a bubble that goes from one side to the next and if that bubble remains in the center, then the object or space is leveled properly.

Note that some of the newer models of refrigerators function much better than the older ones, but leveling is almost always beneficial to your RV's refrigerator.

Things Not Staying in One Spot

Being on level ground means you have level countertops and objects are not moving from one end to the other inside the RV. Objects won't fall over or fly around in the RV, especially if they are mounted (which can make for some rather deadly projectiles). With a surface that is not level, you might be fighting to keep the coffee mug from sliding off the table, having a nice meal with the food looking like it wants to escape from your plate, and other such inconveniences.

Lack of Sleep

When the RV is not leveled, you might find it difficult to get a good night's sleep. We are used to sleeping on level ground and a tilted level feels alien to us. Plus, there is the problem of rolling off your bed, into the wall, into another person, or just moving around as though your body is somehow figure skating in your sleep. None of the aforementioned situations sound like they could contribute to a blissful sleep.

Wrong Water Tank Levels

Most RVs come with water tank readers that let you know the current level of your water. With a tilt, they could show a shortage of water, sending you into panic mode because you just filled the freshwater tank recently. Now, you are needlessly worried about a possible leak in the tank or that you hadn't actually bought enough water.

Damage to the Slide-Outs

People often think slide-outs are sturdy and strong. While that may be true, they are still affected by the same forces that made the apple fall from the tree into Newton's lap. Yes, we are talking about gravity. Fun fact: the whole scenario of Newton sitting under the apple tree and discovering gravity is a myth.

But back to the point I am trying to make. If the RV is not level, the slide-outs will apply pressure on one side of the RV. This causes damage to that side, affecting the mechanisms that operate the slide-outs.

WHAT TO DO IF THE RV BREAKS DOWN

Spending a night stranded on the side of the road does not contribute to the adventure you had planned for yourself or your family, which is why you should keep the below tips in mind.

Prevention Is Better Than Repair

Make sure you are performing routine maintenance and check-ups on your RV. Do not leave your motorhome unattended for a long time. Through check-ups, you can discover any problem before it worsens. You must be aggressive when you are working on preventive care. It's either that, or looking embarrassingly in your side mirror as your RV is billowing smoke through a nice neighborhood and the folks nearby are throwing some rather colorful language your way. In all honesty, a broken-down RV is a danger to you, as well as the people who are in close proximity to the vehicle.

When Trouble Comes Knocking at the Door

In a perfect world, inspections are all it takes to keep trouble at bay, but we are not in a perfect world and, well, excrement happens (this is strictly a PG-13 book). Here, we are going to assume the inevitable has happened. So what do you do? How can you deal with the scenario?

If a breakdown occurs, it could happen in any form ranging from an empty gas tank to a wobbly wire to other mechanical failures indicated by terrifying noises you know should not be coming out of any vehicle, let alone one you live in. In such cases, if you can keep driving, then do so until you have reached a safe place to park your motorhome, whether that place is a truck shop, RV camp, or a wide open space. During this process, take it slow. Put on your hazard lights and move to one side of the road, allowing the traffic to pass you by. If you start smelling something funky, make sure you find a spot to pull over as quickly as possible.

Keep your RV as far off the road as possible without tipping it over into a ravine or getting the tires stuck in soft mud. If you have people with you and they look at you with expressions of concern, stay calm. This will assure them there is nothing major to be concerned about.

Do the traffic a favor and set up cones or reflector triangles to divert them to a safer lane. You can also use flares for this purpose, but if there is an oil leak, skip this step.

Do your family a favor by not getting run over while you are setting up stuff on the road.

Keep the hazard lights on and if you have some reflective clothing, put it on. Have some for your family and make them wear it as well.

Once you have ensured the RV is parked to the side of the road and you, your family, and your pets are all safe, you can then call for backup. If you are one of those people who has spent considerable time in the garage, you might already know what to do about the problem. But, like most of us, you might be out-matched by the complexity of the problem. In this case, don't try and fix anything yourself. Let the help arrive and take over.

Calling Support

Remember when I mentioned a few apps you should have with you? Well, make sure that along with those apps, you also have the phone numbers and contact details of nearby RV assistance programs or establishments.

On the off-chance that you cannot find the number of the local help, then either call 9-1-1 if there is an emergency, or take a cab to the nearest town to look for support. If you can find a gas or service station nearby, reach out to them for help. Usually, if the problem is small, then they might be able to take care of it easily.

You could also sign up for roadside assistance or RV insurance, which we shall look at a later chapter. However, keep in mind something important—make sure that when you are signing up for such roadside assistance, you check the below criteria:

- They have nationwide coverage
- They have the type of towing facilities that can tow the RV you have. Imagine signing up for assistance and realizing they can't tow your RV for repairs—that's going to be a bummer.

Service Centers

Now, let us suppose that you have not signed up for any assistance. This is where connectivity comes in as you can easily look online for the nearest service center.

If connectivity is an issue in the area you're visiting, make sure you have saved the numbers of all the essential service centers along the roads you are taking. This technique of saving the numbers of service centers works both for when you have a planned journey, as well as if you are being spontaneous. Here's why:

If your journey is planned, then all you have to do is store the numbers beforehand.

If you are trying to be spontaneous, you still typically decide where to go before you get into the RV. Whenever you choose your destination, quickly check online for all the service centers along the way and make a note of their contact details before hitting the road.

But honestly, I prefer that you are always prepared for any emergency. Keep contacts of these service centers or repair shops so you are not left stranded in the middle of an empty highway—that looks like it could be the setting for a new horror show—without any idea of what to do next.

ELECTRICITY AND POWER

Most of us here aren't electrical engineers. However, if you just so happen to be one, you might be tempted to skip this chapter with a confident smile on your face, thinking, "Pfft! I already know whatever he is about to say."

However, I still recommend you read this chapter so you can understand the basics of RV electricity and power, and how your expertise can be put to use.

Importance of Power

Essentially, one of the things you should remember when you are thinking about your RV's power is a formula: watts, which signifies the total power, is a result of current, the product of amps and volts. If you transfer the statement into an equation, it's written as: watts = amps x volts, or $W = A \times V$.

The above formula will help you manage the number of electrical devices you have plugged in at any point in your RV. You could potentially use all the electrical devices you have, as long as they are within the limit of the total wattage. However, if you cross the limit, then you might just trip the circuit. That means interrupting a plot twist in the movie you were watching in the RV—definitely not something you would want to happen.

Read up about the total wattage of your RV. You can find this information in your vehicle's manual. When you are using electrical appliances, check how much power is needed for each appliance. This way, you can find out if you have to turn off some electrical devices before plugging in another. You really don't want your RV to shut down because you were making coffee.

One for Two

Your RV comes with two different types of electrical systems:

- A 12-volt electrical system
- A 120-volt electrical system

The 12-volt electrical system is typically powered by a single battery, but that may not be the case as some RVs have multiple batteries powering the system. This system is responsible for running your refrigerator, your water heater, your water pump, most of the lights in your RV, and many other vital components. The 120-volt electrical system, on the other hand, is used for other devices plugged into outlets, such as the television, kitchen appliances, phone chargers, or computer power cords. The 120-volt system is usually powered by a generator.

In the end, both systems need to be charged whenever you get the opportunity. But how can you charge them? It all comes down to the power cord.

30 Amp or 50 Amp

Most RVs come with a power cord you can use to plug in to an electrical charging outlet, which can be found at most camps. The cords come in two forms, 30-amp and 50-amp.

A 30-amp power cord has three prongs and the 50-amp comes with four. At this point, the statement "the more the merrier" couldn't be truer. The 50-amp cord, with its four prongs, provides more power than a 30-amp cord.

When you enter an RV campground, you might be able to find a charging station for both the 30-amp and 50-amp cord types. But in many camps, there may not be an option for the 50. It is for this reason that I recommend having an adapter to convert a 50-amp to a 30-amp. However, if you are using an adapter, be aware of an important point. Even though you are using a 50, converting it into a 30-amp cord means you are generally going to get the same power a 30 does, rather than getting the entire power of the 50. This is why it is always prudent to make a note of your electrical appliances and gadgets. You can find out how to use them in any situation you are presented with.

Don't Just Plug In

Your phone or laptop has been switched off for a long time. You cannot wait to get them both started so you can access your work, visit your social platforms for a quick update, or just know you are still connected to the Internet. You spot a camp, and in that camp, you see the charging station. At that point, you know how the people who first discovered fire might have felt.

So you park your RV and get the plug out to charge your vehicle.

But hold on there just a minute. There are a few things you need to know before you plug in.

- First, check if the campground's electrical wiring is safe. The easiest way to do this is by using a polarity tester. You can find these relatively inexpensive devices at most electrical stores. The polarity tester will let you know if there is a potential for any or all of the electrical components of your RV to get fried.
- Next, make sure you switch off all electricity in your RV.
- Once you have done that, you can then plug in the power cord. Make sure the connection is secure before you switch on the charge.

- If you have the budget, you can consider investing in surge guards. They are an extra precaution against a sudden surge of power to your systems.
- Finally, you can start charging your RV.

Solar Power

Those who have the necessary investment capabilities may want to think about using solar panels to power the RV. However, make sure you are aware of the weather in your area. If you have sufficient sunlight, adding solar panels might benefit you.

Many RVers who enjoy boondocking or camping in the wilderness where there are no charging capabilities often make use of solar panels to supply their vehicles with the required power.

RV Insurance

Stuff happens. And when you have coverage, you can turn to your insurance company to take care of the necessary expenses. The question is, how do you choose the best insurance for your RV? What companies should you trust?

Here are a few tips to keep in mind when checking out the insurance:

- Take your time when you are looking for insurance. You can go directly to an insurance company to ask for more details, as well as look for specialty brokers or agents. They have a wealth of information that can help you be sure of your decision. Check online for reviews about insurance companies, however, note that people often give low reviews because they are either disgruntled or they did not read the fine print before signing on for something. Find other sources of information to learn more about RV insurance companies even if you have to seek advice from your friends or family who might have knowledge about this topic. In fact, try to get in touch with the RV community. Word-of-mouth information is valuable and might point you in the right direction.

- Make sure you and the insurance company have the same value for your RV before you buy the insurance. This ensures that if a loss does occur at some point, the cash value the insurance company places on your RV aligns with what you had in mind.
- Double and triple check all the coverage you are getting. You don't want to buy insurance and then later realize some parts are missing. Also, look for any additional benefits provided by the company or institution.
- Many insurers will adjust your premium based on where you store your RV. Make sure you have stored your RV in a safe environment, and do not lie about this to your insurance company.
- If you have a decent no-claims bonus on an existing vehicle, you can actually mirror this onto your second vehicle (which is your RV). For that to happen, you obviously need to have existing insurance on another vehicle that you own.
- Reach out to agents or companies who are extremely knowledgeable about RVs. Most people make the mistake of getting an insurance from an entity with limited knowledge of RVs, only to realize they were not covered for their losses because certain things were not clear in the claim.
- Make sure you let the insurance company know that you are going to use your RV as a home, if you are planning that. This

allows them to cover the personal belongings you have, as they fall under full-time coverage.
- If you would like, you can even cover roadside assistance, but that may require a little more spending. However, think about this option and compare it to all the roadside assistance companies the insurance companies work with.

RVer Health Insurance

At the end of the day, your health matters, so protect it as much as you can. You can make use of RVer health insurance options provided by many companies. However, use the tips provided in the previous section to find the right insurance for you.

Remember, due diligence is the new prudence. I completely made that up, but you get the point.

After all of the preparations made for your RV, it is time to look into the actual journey. More importantly, getting to know more about camping, boondocking, and other important components of the RV lifestyle.

CHAPTER 5
Camping and Boondocking Basics

I F YOU ARE new to camping, then the idea of 'boondocking' might sound rather alien to you. However, if you have been researching it, you might have some idea of what it is. Either way, it is best to find out more about the various activities for your RV.

In other words, get ready for the fun stuff.

WHAT IS BOONDOCKING ALL ABOUT?

When you are boondocking, you are camping without any hookups. What do I mean by hookups? Well, the term is used to refer to water, electricity, or sewer facilities. Boondocking means you are planning to go off the grid.

Basically, it is the idea that you get off the highway and stay at free locations without the presence of too many amenities or only use amenities when and if they are available.

The main purpose of boondocking is to disconnect yourself from the electrical or virtual world, make time for yourself, and simply enjoy your surroundings. This is probably one of the most popular reasons for RVing—the idea that you can immerse yourself in nature without thinking about all the things you consider important in your real life (such as phones and internet connection).

Boondocking can also be possible while you are connected as well. Boondockers prefer national parks where they can park for free.

HOW TO CAMP FOR FREE ALL OVER THE WORLD

One of the important things to consider before you begin boondocking is to check for more information about camping sites. Research thoroughly where you are allowed to park for free, and where you might have to pay a certain fee for keeping an RV parked for an extended period. Typically, anything outside city limits is available without restrictions, but that also depends on the local laws.

Here are the rules on camping or boondocking in various places around the world:

North America

Across the continent, there are hundreds of places where you can camp for free. All you need to do is be aware of where these locations are. You could use the apps I provided earlier, or you can make use of www.freecampsites.net to check out places where you can park for free.

Apart from that, you should know that public lands are not always free, but there are often dispersed camping areas close to these public lands. Knowing about these areas is important because they allow you to camp for free. To find out more about these dispersed lands, you can perform your own little online search or use the website www.recreation.gov.

This might come as a surprise to you, but you can also use Walmart parking lots to camp overnight for free. However, make sure you are not sleeping outside or pitching a tent, not only because it is not allowed in some areas, but also for your own safety. Additionally, try not to stay in the parking lot for too long. Some people end up staying for two weeks and ruin the experience for other RVers.

Mexico, Central and South America

Apart from a few sites, you are not going to find a lot of free camping spots in Mexico. For those that are available, you can find them thanks to the charity of the locals, through word-of-mouth information, or because of your own sense of adventure. An important thing to note is that if you are planning to camp somewhere, you have to learn about the local area. Make sure you are safe and are aware of your surroundings. I would recommend www.ontheroadin.com/rv-mexico-2/ if you are looking for camping spots, but most, if not all, will require you to pay.

Central and South America have quite a few options if you are looking for free spots to camp. One of the things you can do is find a hostel and ask if you could use their parking spot. They might allow you to use it for free or for a modest fee. The Central American border crossings can be quite dangerous, so try and plan your trip in advance if you intend to cross borders. In many cases, the locals are quite helpful and may point you in the direction of free campsites. You can always check out national and local parks as they either offer camping there for free or for a truly paltry fee.

Fortunately for many campers, wild camping is quite prevalent in many areas in Central and South America. Wild camping basically means that you find a spot and put down a tent wherever you are. Especially in Central and South America, there are many landscapes that make this type of camping truly worth it. You can usually find free camping (called "camping libre" or "camping agreste" in the local language) or low-cost private campgrounds in cities and the countryside.

iOverlander (www.ioverlander.com) is a great resource to find such areas where you can locate camping grounds to set up your tent. However, the platform does not provide the price of setting up camps, which is usually a really small fee, so you may have to research a location before you head there.

Europe

Much of Europe can be your camping playground, however, there are still restrictions in certain areas.

One thing to note is that Europe has an abundance of backpackers, wild campers, and RVers. You might have a little trouble in Greece since camping for free is actually illegal, but it turns out no one really cares about that and you can often find campers setting up tents and other vehicles in some areas. Do note that you cannot stay for long in these areas as it might draw the attention of the local authorities. While the authorities are not strict, they still might enforce the law if they discover you have been in one location for too long (this makes them suspicious).

But when it comes to other parts of Europe, you can find campgrounds either within the cities or on the outskirts. And, of course, they are free! In fact, many of the camping options in Europe are just as beautiful as the ones in North America. There are many other campgrounds that might require you to pay, but the sights are worth it.

Make sure you are following the rules of the region. Some areas do not allow noise levels to be high beyond a certain time limit. That means no shouting, "I'm king of the world!" after midnight.

Australia and New Zealand

Similar to North America, you can find numerous camping grounds and national parks littered throughout Australia. While you are more likely to run into low-cost camping grounds, that does not mean free camping grounds are not available. You could also make use of truck stops, rest areas, and numerous parking lots. However, you may not be allowed to stay there for long, depending on the area and location. If you are not certain about an area, then make sure you learn more about it before setting up for the night. You could be fined $200 or more for parking in areas not meant for camping. Many RVers have made the mistake of blindly assuming an area allows them to park their motorhomes. WikiCamps has been recommended as one of the best apps to find various camping sites around Australia (including our favorite type: FREE).

New Zealand also offers many options for camping. Check out this website—www.camping_nz.rankers.co.nz/filters/campgrounds—to look for camping sites for your RV throughout the country.

Alternatively, you can use the app Spaceships, which provides camping info and sites in both Australia and New Zealand.

Africa

While free camping is definitely available, it is not common. You might find that most grounds are protected by the local authorities, as they are highly wary of poachers and illegal hunting activities.

But more importantly, the thing you should be concerned about is not whether there is a campground (because camping in Africa is quite common), but rather, the wildlife. You are going to be surrounded by all kinds of animals and creatures. If you are not prepared or are unaware of the local terrain, you might find yourself unable to deal with local wildlife, which includes elephants, baboons, hyenas, lions, tigers, and rhinos. And these are just the creatures you can see. Mosquitos, snakes, and other wildlife are present throughout Africa. However, the country also boasts some of the most incredible sights you may come across. Your best bet is to find a local guide, or someone who is familiar with the place you are camping in, who can talk to the local tribes (whom you might have to pay for using camping grounds) and give you important tips on navigating through the terrain and dealing with the wildlife.

Once again, you can refer to iOverlander to look at numerous camping locations submitted by other users. You should still perform your own research, though, before venturing into any of the camps.

Asia

If I start talking about Asia in detail, I might need an entire book. Or maybe two. But I will try and cover those areas where camping is most prevalent.

China

There are not a lot of campsites and grounds in China. Part of the reason for this is that the culture in the country does not believe in or indulge in the idea of RVing around the country or camping in general. That being said, there are a few camping sites you can make use of for free. For example, tour operators set up camping colonies near the Great Wall.

I would recommend that you do not camp too close to the cities, or you might attract too much attention. Try to blend in and stay in lower lying areas away from roads, lakes, and more traveled areas. You can try to ask locals for help and, in quite a few cases, you may be invited into their homes.

The last piece of advice I can give you is that if you do get caught, then play dumb. You are a foreigner. You didn't know about the rules. You have never come across such information. Who are you again?

Tibet, Mongolia, and Singapore

You are not going to find free camping areas in these countries. In fact, Singapore has no areas where you can camp without paying a fee. Mongolia might be a bit more lenient on camping activities, but you will likely need a guide to show you where you can wild camp. Typically, nobody troubles you, as long as you are not causing them any inconvenience.

Southeast Asia: Thailand, Malaysia, Vietnam, Cambodia, Laos

These countries are similar to Mongolia. Nobody bothers you if you do not bother them. Make sure you are aware of the local laws and the good practices. There are many spots to camp, but you might find that the local insect population could be a pain in the nether region. Research about fauna and what you can do to prevent infections and diseases.

RV CLUBS AND MEMBERSHIPS

When in doubt, join a club. The benefits of being part of a community are many. You get to know about all the campsites and their details. You have a group of people who share the same passion as you. Practically any piece of information one could ever need about RVing is at your fingertips. You can make informed decisions about insurance, locations, journeys, support services, or other various important requirements for your RV life.

There are many clubs you can be a part of. I have narrowed down a few for you to consider.

Passport America

This club is ideal for those who wish to camp for more than just a few nights in a year. You might be able to save a lot of money on camping fees and facilities. The app has over 1,800 participating campgrounds as part of their network, so you can get discounts at various locations across the country.

One of the great features of the app is that you can actually check prices, discounts, amenities, pictures, and any discount restrictions on all participating campgrounds on the main page itself. This allows you to decide if you would really like to be a member of the club.

Escapees RV Club

What makes Escapees RV Club attractive is the fact that they cater to both newbies and professional RVers. As a member, you can access numerous support groups and discounts. The stand-out feature is that they offer RV classes, which you can take either in person or online. Each of these classes helps you to familiarize yourself with your vehicle, learn to troubleshoot, journey in comfort, and essentially learn all the important tips and tricks of your RV.

They have over 1,000 participating campsites across the country, and discounts range anywhere from 15 to 50%.

Escapees also provides you with Rainbow Parks. These are parks that let you choose from different camping options: short-term, long-term, leases, and deeded lots for sale. Currently, there are seven Rainbow Parks, located in Alabama, Arizona, Florida, Missouri, New Mexico, Tennessee, and Texas. These parks are rather upscale because they offer a lot of amenities along with just parking space. You have access to laundromats, supermarkets, dog parks, and so much more.

Good Sam Club

This is a rather popular club even though they only offer 10 to 30% discounts. The main reason for this is that they have over 2,400 participating campsites. So while they don't provide higher discounts than the other clubs on this list, they do include plenty of options to choose from. For an extra fee, they also provide roadside assistance for your RV, along with other features, such as tire and wheel protection, insurance, and additional services. New RVers would greatly benefit from this club because of the discounts they can get for buying essential products from one of the club's partners, Camping World. This includes protective clothing and gear, propane tanks, supplies, and more.

LONG-TERM AND SHORT-TERM PARKING OPTIONS FOR YOUR RV

Going into long-term RVing means finding spots where you can park your RV, either for a long term, where you are planning on staying in that particular location for a few months, or short-term, where you would like to be there for longer than just a few days, but still intend to leave for another location soon.

What you should look at is not just the duration of your stay, but other features as well. Let me show you what I mean.

Long-Term Stays

Once you have decided that a long-term stay is indeed the option for you, you have to figure out just where you are going to park that giant beast of a vehicle. While you are considering this, you might also want to think about some other important stuff.

Since you are planning to live long-term, are you okay being a part of nature? Or would you prefer to have access to amenities? Would you like to be located in areas that offer certain activities, like hiking or watching a movie at the local cinema? Do you want to be a part of a community?

The reason you have to ask yourself the above questions is because staying somewhere for a longer period of time means you may like to have certain aspects of your normal life as part of your RV lifestyle. So think about the place you would like to live in. For example, do you enjoy surfing and kayaking? Are you the kind of person who enjoys hiking? Additionally, would you like to have certain conveniences nearby, such as a laundromat, gym, or a grocery store? Do you feel more comfortable with a pharmacy close to you? Would you like to participate in local community centers or churches?

All of these questions might help you figure out where you would like to stay. You can choose from the many RV parks available throughout the country—you'll actually find that many RV parks offer long-term discounts. You might not necessarily find them on the websites, however, so your best bet is to actually get in touch with these parks and try to negotiate a deal.

Many of the long-term RV parks will offer monthly rates at a few hundred dollars and will also provide you with additional amenities, like electricity, water, and possibly sewer, cable, and WiFi. Of course, the way these amenities are available may also vary from park to park. For example, some parks offer "free WiFi" that is so crowded, you might as well send carrier pigeons to Google headquarters to get your information faster.

Short-Term Stays

You don't really have to worry too much about short-term stays. There are many options you can make use of, including dedicated apps (that were mentioned earlier) to find nearby short-term RV parks. However, I would also recommend that you get the app, "Oh, Ranger! Park Finder." This is a truly useful tool because it is a complete database of every national and state park in the U.S. This means no matter where you are, you can find the closest RV park to you. One of the other features of the app is that it includes information about each park, as well as activities you can take part in while you're there.

I would also recommend that even if you find such RV parks, it is best if you call them directly and see if you can get any discounts or benefits for your RV stay. Most of these parks don't like to advertise their promotions and offers, so you might have to do a little bit of legwork to get this information.

CHAPTER 6
Making Money on the Road

How much money do you think you will need for your RV on a monthly basis?

$4,000? $10,000? $15,000, if you are planning to live in upscale areas and using expensive features?

Regardless of what amount you think you need, there might be one thought that comes to your head—how am I going to get money while I travel?

It is nice to look at travel blogs, BuzzFeed, or other such websites and see how easy it is for many people to find jobs, but it doesn't always work that way. You might also come across blogs where people claim to have saved (insert insane saving amount here) while they were traveling. All you need to do is purchase their quick guide for $49.99.

Let's not kid ourselves. If someone knew the secret formula for success and saving money, they would not be selling it online. Have you ever heard Elon Musk come on an advertisement and say, "For just $349.99, you get to know all the secrets of getting a machine to the moon! Limited offer only. Terms and conditions apply."

But do not despair, this does not mean you cannot find sources of income while you are on your RV journey. Here are some ways you can look for work to get yourself some cash.

FINDING SEASONAL WORK

One of the best parts about seasonal work is that there is always demand for temporary labor. By keeping pace with the seasons, you can find temporary work as a camping guide, on boats, in bars or restaurants, and many other places.

Here are a few types of seasonal jobs that are usually available:

Retail

You might come across stores with a "help wanted" sign on their front. This is the easiest way to find retail jobs that are seasonal. One of the best ways to do this is to walk around a mall or downtown and stop in to fill out applications. But this also means you'll need to find an RV park close to a mall and other shopping amenities. When you are looking for jobs, make sure you and your employer are clear about your work duration. You wouldn't want them thinking you are going to work there for at least four months when you are planning on leaving after month two.

You can also check out local job portals to get an idea of other temporary work available in the area you are in.

Temps

You can also make use of temp agencies looking for temporary work to fill in for staff who have gone on holiday. Making use of portals, such as Manpower, Snelling & Snelling, and Kelly Services, will allow you to quickly search for temp jobs in the area. Temping is an industry that has always shown growth and for that reason, there is usually no shortage of jobs.

Delivery

Logistical and delivery companies often need more staff during certain seasons. One such example is UPS, who actually have options to hire for seasonal work, as they could always use the extra help. You could also look at the DHL website to find out about seasonal delivery work.

But delivery does not have to be restricted to just parcels and packages. Many restaurants and fast food chains are usually posting job openings for food delivery positions as well. This also goes for certain ecommerce businesses, like Amazon.

Outdoors

When we talk about working outdoors, we are talking about resorts and public areas. These places are always looking for additional help not only for their activity areas, but for the restaurants, bars, and other facilities they offer.

Many of the hospitality, travel, and tourism agencies and companies offer numerous seasonal job opportunities you can take advantage of.

Finding Seasonal Work

Of course, having such jobs available is one thing, but finding them is another. As mentioned earlier, you can take a walk around the local mall to look for job openings.

However, one of the most effective ways to find work is to look into job portals. There are plenty of options for you. Some of the popular ones are Indeed.com, LinkUp.com, SimplyHired.com, and CoolWorks.com. The reason for their popularity is their advanced search function that allows you to specifically look for seasonal jobs. You can also use keywords and narrow down the location to your area to look for jobs around you. By simply typing, "seasonal," "seasonal holiday," "seasonal retail," "seasonal summer," or any other appropriate keyword brings up numerous listings.

In some cases, you can look at the job listings and, rather than send applications through the website, you can get in touch with the companies directly.

Other websites I can recommend you look into are Seasonworkers.com and SummerJobs.com.

WHY FREELANCE WORK MIGHT BE RIGHT FOR YOU

The best thing about freelance work is that the job satisfaction is entirely up to you. The reason freelancing work is on the rise nowadays is because of the flexible working hours that provide freelancers a healthier work-life balance. This balance is something you might be looking for, especially if you are traveling in an RV.

Still, there are a few things to think about before entering freelance work.

Your Working Hours Are Yours

When you are working as a freelancer, you can choose the hours you put into your work. This will depend on the project you are working on and how many different projects you can handle at one time. You can balance the hours you put in based on your work strategy. For example, you can work constantly for seven days a week and then take a three-day break. The way you work depends entirely on you. You could even put in 12 to 15 hours per day for four days and completely unwind for the remaining three days. The scheduling of your job is entirely up to you.

There is no paid vacation when you are working as a freelancer, but there is such a thing as taking time off and not answering to anyone.

You Are the Accounts Person

When you are freelancing, then you have to be the one to chase after the money owed to you. It's your responsibility to negotiate your working rates, and even if your work delivers incredible value, you may have to be able to justify the cost. Additionally, it is also up to you to reject or confirm extra requests. When you hear phrases such as, "Just take a look at something," or "Give it a quick glance," it usually means, "Can you do this for free?" and "When you start taking a quick glance, I am going to add more tasks to your plate." This means you really need to have a thick skin (metaphorically speaking) to navigate the world of freelance working and pay negotiations.

You Are on Your Own

While you could join a freelancing community and seek assistance from other freelancers, for the most part, you are on your own. You cannot rely on coworkers or team members to help you out during a fix. If there is a challenge that awaits you, then you are the one who will eventually deal with it.

With that being said, are you willing to do freelance work? Here are some places where you can find freelance work:

- Upwork
- Guru

- Freelancer.com
- Mechanical Turk
- Toptal (most of the work here is geared towards finance and software development, but check it out and see if there are opportunities within your field)
- Fiverr
- Freelancermap.com (focuses on IT projects only)
- FlexJobs
- People Per Hour
- OnSite
- iFreelance

It is always better to look at multiple platforms, as that allows you to check out a plethora of jobs in the market before you narrow down your options to just one.

WORKING AT THE CAMPGROUND

Does the idea of finding a job that is dog-friendly, rent-free, and outdoors sound appealing to you? Do you think such a job could not exist? Well, that is exactly what you get when you work in an RV campground.

Campground hosts, or workampers, manage campgrounds across the country. In many occasions, they actually offer free tent and RV space in exchange for the work. You could be doing something rather simple, such as greeting guests, answering questions, doing routine maintenance, light cleaning, and possibly collecting campground fees. In return, you can get to use the campground facilities and spaces free of charge.

Alternatively, if you are looking for a paid job, you can find that as well, but you won't be able to enjoy the other free benefits provided by the campgrounds.

Every campsite is unique and offers its own set of services and work opportunities. For the most part, these are simple jobs you won't have to stress about too much. However, the drawback to that is you won't be earning enough to have extra spending capabilities. If you are indeed looking at the amount of pay you get in return, then make sure you are focused on freelancing work or other kinds of temporary employment.

HOW TO START EARNING PASSIVE INCOME ONLINE

There is one rule when you are thinking of earning passive income, which is there are no get-rich-quick schemes. If you have come across someone who is trying to make you buy some incredible money-earning mechanism, then you have officially come across a snake oil salesman.

But that doesn't mean it isn't possible to earn passive income online. You can, but you still have to put in the effort to make it happen.

Here are some ways you can earn passive income:

Try Out Index Funds

Index funds provide you with a way to invest in the stock market that is completely passive. For example, if you put your money into an index fund based on the S&P 500 Index, you will be investing in the general market. This way, you have to look at how the market functions over a certain period of time, and then you can earn money back on your investment. However, do note that in the world of investments, the lower the risk, the lower the payoff, so you can't expect to spend a certain amount of money and then walk away with a million dollars. Sure, those things happen in movies, but movies never show all the steps that led to the eventual earning of said million dollars.

Make YouTube Videos

These days, almost everyone wants to make videos on YouTube. The sheer number of content creators is just astounding. If you would like to start a YouTube channel for a particular topic, chances are there already exists a channel (or even multiple channels) all about that specific thing. This means you are probably going to be competing with other, more established, content creators on the platform. But don't let that deter you from starting your own channel.

The main attraction of YouTube lies in the variety of content available for you to work with, ranging from gaming to food to travel. You can create videos for just about any area you would like—music, tutorials, opinions, comedy, movie reviews—and then put them online.

But wait, how does one earn money through YouTube? The setup is fairly simple, you just link Google AdSense to the videos. This will create advertisement overlays and allow promoters to use your channel to show their video ads. There are so many different kinds of ad formats these promoters can use.

The main thing to note is not just any channel can start showing ads on their videos. There are certain criteria you need to meet:

- You need to become part of the YouTube Partner Program

- You need to have accumulated at least 4,000 hours of video watch-time for your videos within the past 12 months
- You need to have at least 1,000 subscribers on your channel

Sure, that does sound like a lot of work, but the payoff is usually good. And besides, you are making videos on things you enjoy.

Affiliate Marketing

You've probably seen this term thrown around a lot these days. You might wonder, is this another scam by people who simply want to target desperate people? Not so. Sure, there are many scams revolving around affiliate marketing, but almost all of them come into the "get this secret technique for X amount of dollars" category.

Affiliate marketing is real, and just about anybody can do it. Here is how it works:

You first have to find a portal that allows you to sign up for affiliate marketing. You then promote certain products or services on your site, for which you will be paid either a flat fee or a percentage of the amount of the resulting sale.

Let's take an example right here. You head over to Amazon (one of the popular platforms for affiliate marketing) and notice a company called AirBrushed (totally made that name up, by the way) selling a new kind of bladeless fans. They are looking for people to promote their products. You sign up on Amazon for affiliate marketing and choose AirBrushed's bladeless fans as the product you would like to market. You then receive a link. You put that link on your website or on your YouTube channel, and that's it. Now, everytime someone clicks on your link and makes a purchase, you get a small percentage of the sale, or a fixed amount in return. Why? Because you were responsible for the sale of said product.

Of course, the whole trick is to market the product so people can click into it, but that is essentially the gist of the entire affiliate marketing program.

And it is completely legal. In fact, as I mentioned earlier, Amazon is a popular option for affiliate marketing.

Photography

Do you enjoy taking pictures? Consider uploading all your photos on websites such as Shutterstock and iStockphoto. That way, if anyone comes across your image and downloads it, you get a small percentage as a commission.

And that's just for one photo. As you begin to upload more and more, you increase the opportunities and channels of cash flow source. This is because your photos can be sold again and again. You simply need to create your photo portfolio, put it on one or more platforms, and then start passively earning money on the photos downloaded.

Write an eBook

The one drawback to this is the fact that it takes a lot of time, initially, to write your ebook. But once you have done so, you can publish it, market it, and begin earning money on its purchase. Of course, the marketing is another aspect that might take a while, but the rewards are plentiful if you succeed.

There are many self-publishing platforms you can take advantage of. Obviously, Amazon is popular for self-publishers. You simply have to send across your book for review and once it has passed the test, it becomes available on the platform. After that, you can get your friends and family to purchase the book and provide a rating on it. Each purchase and rating helps you get your ebook to a better position, thereby increasing your sales even more.

Sell Your Products on the Internet

If you have a special skill, why not sell your creations online? Do you enjoy pottery? Are you a skilled painter? Enjoy making mittens? Whatever you do can be sold online.

In today's world, finding a place where you can reach a wide audience is not difficult. It is the work that goes into marketing your products that is challenging. If you have been on Instagram, then you already know the platform is made for people looking to sell what they create, from fancy art collectibles to cute toys to even clothing and apparel. In fact, you could partner up with a local business, create an online platform for them, and market their products while earning a commission through your work.

If you are good at something, then you can create your own set of instruction or lesson videos and then sell them online. You can use platforms such as Udemy (by far the most popular one) to create courses for people and earn money every time someone buys those courses.

Invest in Real Estate

This is not exactly a way to earn passive income. In fact, you could say that it is semi-passive. However, once you have established the property and maintained it well, it is really only a matter of marketing it properly.

Of course, the downside to all of this is you may need to come up with the initial investment and, based on the property, this could be a small or large amount. But the good thing about real estate is that you can invest in a wide variety of properties based on your budget and requirements. For example, you can invest in apartments, condos, villas, small houses, large houses, and any other type of property you think you are capable of investing in and maintaining.

Additionally, there are professional property managers who can manage your real estate investments for you, usually for around 10% of the monthly rent. These professional managers can help you make your investment more passive (since they will be putting in most of the hard work), but will take a bite out of your returns. My recommendation is to know all the details about the agent before you consider working with them.

Rent Out Your Home

You can even rent out your home to people who would like to live there temporarily. You can list your property on short-term rental platforms, such as Airbnb. People will use your property for as long as they have booked it online and then move on.

You will need to have someone around to help maintain the house while you are gone, but you can easily do this by enlisting the help of someone you know and paying them for their efforts.

Of course, the drawback to this is that you are going to be allowing complete strangers into your home. You might not know about their character or behavior. However, most platforms (such as Airbnb) allow you to first get in touch with the guests and talk to them before you agree to anything. This way, you can be comforted by knowing that the person staying in your home is not someone who might destroy anything.

Silent Partnership

Do you know of a business that is in need of some capital? If that is indeed the case, then you can become an angel investor in that business. But rather than offering your capital in the form of a loan, you can purchase an equity position in the business. This means you earn revenue based on the profit-sharing rules put into place. The business owner will, of course, take care of the business, but you will be earning eventual profits because of your investment.

CHAPTER 7
Solo RVing Done Right

THERE IS SOMETHING magnificent about solo adventuring. In fact, you might have seen the recent trend where people prefer to travel the world on their own. They save up for a long time, plan out their journey, pack their bags, and off they go. They enjoy every aspect, like finding an exotic location, experiencing the local food, being a part of many adventures, and simply discovering more things by themselves.

Solo adventure is 'the thing' these days.

The same applies for solo RVing. It is similar to traveling alone as a backpacker. The only difference is that you are traveling on board a moving home with a lot of comforts thrown in.

DON'T LET BEING BY YOURSELF STOP YOU!

Solo traveling is not a lonely experience. Many people might say otherwise, but there is something liberating about experiencing the world on your own.

However, taking on the journey all by yourself can be a pretty intimidating task. After all, you have to figure out a lot of the stuff by yourself, but this does not have to be the case (hint: you have this book).

First, we are going to dispel a few fears of solo RVing.

It's Not Safe

Solo RVing presents the same types of risks that group traveling does. However, there are a few advantages of solo RVing—there are less chances for human errors, you are not easily distracted, there is less need to make frequent pit stops, and other such scenarios that could develop when you are traveling with others.

But what about the dangers from external sources? I generally think the worries about solo RVing are typically blown out of proportion. People complain about how you could be robbed while on the road. This is not just restricted to solo RVers. People who travel in groups have as much danger of being robbed as people who travel alone. In fact, if you are with someone else, things can even get a bit more complicated because you are now concerned for both yourself and the other person. The news loves to talk about break-ins and thefts by putting the focus on solo traveling, but they fail to cover stories about families and groups who have faced the same problems.

At the same time, you still need to be prepared to face some of these dangers while you are traveling alone. After all, the drawback to it is that you are usually left to fend for yourself, without any assistance. We shall look at some safety techniques you can adopt while you are on the road later in this chapter.

It Can Be Overwhelming

You are going to be in charge of every aspect of taking care of and driving your RV. Checking for maintenance? You are going to be doing that. Washing the tanks? You are responsible for that, and you cannot ask anyone to take over. Meal preparing? Once again, you.

At this point, I might not be painting a nice picture for you to think about when traveling alone. In fact, I might have convinced you to call up any of your old friends whom you haven't kept in touch for years just to accompany you on your journey. You might be willing to pay them, as well.

But that won't be necessary. You see, one of the things about solo RVing are the rewards you can gain from it. You become more independent. You gain confidence since you have to deal with everything. There is also the fact that while things are overwhelming in the beginning, you don't have to handle all of them at the same time.

It's like asking a chef to prepare the starter, main course, dessert, and drinks simultaneously, while also cleaning up the kitchen space and checking for supplies. But what if the same chef was allowed to deal with each task independently?

In a similar manner, you don't have to deal with everything in one go. Take your time to go through the tasks. There is no hurry. After all, you are going to be spending a long time on the road, so take it easy. Let the learning process itself become an adventure.

Loneliness

A lot of people are under the impression that getting into an RV and soloing it around the world can get a bit lonely. However, what separates solo RVing from being part of a crowd is that you can actually interact with people as you see fit. You are free to meet anyone you would like on your journey. Besides, RVing is not exactly a lonely activity. There are tons of social platforms and groups that allow anyone to meet interesting people on their journeys.

You can actually become part of a community by looking for them online. Each stop you make is filled with the pleasure of encountering unique people and making new friends.

Difficult

People sometimes think getting started with solo RVing is more difficult compared to getting started with a group. This is probably because of the idea that only one person will be taking care of the downsizing and preparations. Although this might be true, they forget to think about one important factor—the more people there are in an RV, the more packing you may need to do and the more space-conscious you have to be.

If you are traveling solo, then you are going to have enough space to carry a lot of equipment. Additionally, by traveling solo, you only need to think about what items you need for yourself, eliminating lengthy downsizing processes.

That means no more thinking about whether you need to make more room for your shoes or someone else's. It's your ride. It's your rules.

You are the master of your trip. You are the commander of your vehicle. You are—

Well, you get the point.

STAYING SAFE ON THE ROAD

First things first—stay on the beaten track. Try to follow what others have been doing for years, and don't take unnecessary risks.

Apart from that, here are tips you can take while you are on the road:

- When you are tucking in for the night, make sure you have locked your doors and are aware of where you are parked. If you notice too many beer bottles scattered around in your area, it probably is not a sign of a peaceful place with wonderful people around.
- If you have RV neighbors, let them know you are traveling alone. They will be able to watch out for you.
- Keep your friends and family informed about your route. Let them know where you are, and get some advice if they know about the location you are staying in.
- If you notice that your RV is the only one in the vicinity, there is probably a good reason why. Try to find company.
- If you are staying overnight in a parking lot, stay under a light and, preferably, in front of a security camera. Bonus points for parking next to the security booth.
- Check and see if you are getting good phone reception in the area where you plan to stay. Remember, most horror movie plots take a turn for the worse when the characters know they have lost their phone signals.
- If you feel like something feels "off" about the place you are about to stay in, then trust your instincts.
- When you leave your RV, but are unsure of the neighborhood, close your blinds, lock the vehicle securely, and keep all your valuables inside.
- Keep air horns, alarms, or any other preventive measures in your RV just in case your shouting voice is not too loud.
- There are so many places where you can camp for free, but still remain with a group of RVers.
- If you are taking extra precautions when you are staying with your RV, such as adding locks to all the storage spaces

inside your vehicle, that is a smart move. Do not let anyone convince you that what you are doing is extreme.
- If something is too good to be true, then it usually is.

AVOIDING LONELINESS

Solo travel is fun, there is no denying that. But many people often ponder upon the loneliness that RV traveling can bring.

Now, before we talk about dealing with loneliness, it is important to understand the distinction between being lonely and being alone. On one hand, you have the feeling of being alone. When you are alone, you have either chosen to be in that state or it has happened to you involuntarily. Either way, you are not comfortable with the situation. On the other hand, you have the feeling of loneliness—where you are aware that you are on your own and it has an effect on your emotional and mental state, typically a negative response. One is a state of being, while the other is an emotional response.

Additionally, one has to take into account that certain people are introverted while others are extroverted, which means some people don't mind spending time with themselves while others are social butterflies. In other words, some people rarely go out to meet people and are comfortable boondocking in the woods, away from civilization, while others need to be as close as possible or within the limits of a community, town, city, or other such areas.

So, how are the differences between loneliness and lonesomeness connected to being an introvert or extrovert, especially when it comes to RVing? Simple enough. Introverts can spend time by themselves without being affected by feelings of loneliness. Extroverts might feel lonely when they do not engage with other people for a long time. This is something you have to think about with regards to your RV adventure. Would you like to explore the wilderness and the sights on your own (or with your dog or other pets as company)? Or do you prefer to stop somewhere and get to know the locals?

Once you have decided on your preferred way to enjoy your RV life, then think about how you can keep in touch regardless of where you are. Here are some tips you can follow:

Connection #1: Your Family and Friends

Make sure you do not lose touch with those close to you, whether they are your family, distant cousins, friends, or even Casper the Friendly Ghost (if you happen to know such an entity). When you are connected to people close to you, you are always aware of their presence. You know they are thinking about you, excited to know about your adventures, and are concerned when something happens to you. Additionally, there is a strong bond that keeps you from feeling lonely no matter where you are.

Besides, home is where the heart is. Your RV is your home, but your family and friends are a part of that home even if they are not physically present there.

Connection #2: Join Communities

There are so many RV communities out there to be a part of. Not only can you meet interesting people, but if you happen to make friends in the community, you can find out where their friends are located and drive over to the campground or area they are located in.

Alternatively, you can find out which RV park has a large number of people so you can head over there. There are communities that can help you find out if there are any RV-related events in your area, as well as guide you towards where you want to go next from your current location. Not only that, but they can also inform you of other RVers who have set up their motorhomes in a specific location for a long term, including just how long they have been there.

Communities are not only a great place to meet people, but can also provide some valuable information (as we touched on earlier).

Connection #3: Meet People You Know All Over the Country

There is no rule that says once you are in your RV, all you have to think about is nature, isolation, and cleaning out your black tank once in a while. You are free to go wherever you would like, so try and visit some friends living in other parts of the country. Not only will you experience a wonderful journey along the way, but you may just have a wonderful reunion.

Connection #4: FOMO

Sometimes, when you feel lonely, it might not be because of the lack of people around you. Perhaps it is due to the situation you find yourself in. You might have what people like to refer to as "FOMO," or the "Fear of Missing Out." You could be thinking about:

How your current situation can be much better than it is

The state of your situation as compared to others

You might be wondering if things would be different if you had started a business or if you had simply completed that PhD in university. Perhaps you should have listened to your parents, your boss, your friends, or that voice in your head. All of these thoughts start nagging at you because, for the first time, you actually feel liberated. Our minds are rather funny things. When we are having fun, it automatically starts to think of some rather negative thoughts.

It's as though your mind loves to keep you disappointed. But that is the mind's defense mechanism going into action. It is trying to prevent you from receiving any unpleasant surprises in the future, and so it runs through all the potential scenarios. However, what you must do is be in the present. Don't worry about the "what ifs." Live in the moment.

Don't worry about what other people have. Comparison is the thief of joy. When we compare, we are never going to be content. Eventually, we are going to start feeling different from other people. That, in turn, makes us feel lonely.

Connection #5: Being Absent from the Present

Sometimes, it might not be easy to be in the present. There is a real challenge to living this way because, most often, we are thinking about various situations, people, ideas, and goals.

Try to learn how to keep your mind focused on the present, or what most people would say, in the act of 'mindfulness.' Keep your thoughts from straying away too far from the present day. It is going to be a challenge, but as you get involved in the day-to-day activities of your RV, you will find that it gets much easier. Don't worry too much about the things you have no control over. As you begin to take care of your RV, yourself, the job you have while in the RV, and the community you become a part of, all of the things that make you feel lonely will start dwindling away.

Connection #6: Boredom

Sometimes, you might actually not be lonely, but just bored. If you are unaware of what makes you happy or brings joy to you, then you are often going to feel bored on the road. The trouble with boredom is that one does not easily identify it because thinking that we are bored automatically means our lives are not interesting. And that is a thought most people don't like to have.

There is a simple rule when it comes to boredom, which is to accept that you are feeling bored. This immediately makes things easier because if you can identify the fact that you don't have anything to bring joy or energy into your life at the moment, then you can plan to go get it. You could take a walk outside, read your favorite book, take your dog out for a walk, or get in touch with the RV community to ask them where to find some incredible events or activities. Boredom can easily be treated with simple solutions. Loneliness, on the other hand, is a more complex situation and might require evaluation.

CONNECTING WITH THE COMMUNITY

Finding an RV community is not going to be as challenging as one might think. The world of RV traveling is growing, and you can see evidence of this in the number of campgrounds that have appeared within the past few years. Just by looking at the various special facilities for RVs (there's even an RV resort!), you know there is a tremendous interest in motorhomes. And where there is a huge presence of interest, there might just be a community for that interest.

The world of RVing has no deficiency in the number of communities it offers. You can easily find communities online through a quick search or by using some of the ways provided below to become a part of them.

At the Campground or RV Park

Many campgrounds provide you with the opportunity to meet new people. Not only is the campground itself one big community, but chances are many people staying there are a part of a unique community of their own. This provides you with the chance to make friends, find travel companions, and even get some help, should you need it.

In fact, if you have a problem, chances are that one, or many of the people in the community, has gone through it (especially the experienced RVers) so it would benefit you greatly to become a part of a community.

One of the best ways to meet people is to take a walk around the camp. Find people who are sitting together on camp chairs and join them (you will be surprised at how welcoming they can all be). Strike up conversations with your RV neighbors. Feel free to talk to people. Through your connections, you will be able to either form your own community or become part of another.

Exploring

Whether you are fishing, hiking, or exploring the sights of a tourist attraction, you might just bump into fellow RVers. Take a moment to get to know them. You will be surprised at how simple it can be to connect with others. Of course, you may occasionally get the traveler who prefers to avoid social contact, but do not let that deter you from finding meaningful and incredible connections elsewhere.

During your explorations, you are bound to discover local RV communities in or near the town or city you are staying in.

Online

As I mentioned earlier, you can always find communities online. You can perform your own search, but here are some websites you should check out:

- irv2
- Technomadia
- Wheelingit

We have now covered various aspects of the RV world. However, there are still concerns when it comes to RVing. Let's see if we can deal with those situations.

CHAPTER 8
Commonly Asked Questions

I'S TIME TO "keep it real." Even if RVing is incredible 99% of the time, it is always better to look at the good, the bad, and the ugly of the RV world before heading out on the road.

WHAT IS THE WORST THING ABOUT LIVING IN AN RV?

- Being connected constantly helps you in many ways, but the challenge is to *remain* connected constantly. You might end up in areas where there is no internet connection or mobile service. That results in you trying to find a local café or WiFi hotspot, or worse, looking for the closest area with a connection.
- Be prepared for bad weather. When we are within our homes, the walls are thick so we don't worry about heavy rains or thunderstorms. When you are in an RV, however, the walls are thinner and the weather has a bigger impact.
- The RV maintenance. Sure, there are steps you can follow to make it easier, but it is still work and no one really likes to do that (except maintenance folks, and even they might scowl at the occasional RV-related upkeep work).

- Some RVs have washers and dryers while others, unfortunately, do not. If your RV is not outfitted with the aforementioned machines, you may be surprised to see just how often you find yourself looking for a laundromat.
- Being lonely. We have offered some advice for dealing with that, though, so make sure you use all the tips you can.

WHAT IS THE BEST THING ABOUT RV LIFE?

- You can live by the beach, mountains, desert, lake, or anywhere else you would like. Want to park somewhere close to the Amityville Horror mansion? You can (though in all honesty, why would you?). The freedom to travel to so many places, experiencing so many things, while living on the road is a unique feeling that cannot be described unless you have actually lived it.
- When you are living in an RV, you tend to spend more time outside. You are also motivated to enjoy a healthier life. Many RVers have picked up outdoor hobbies such as hiking, jogging, and rafting. You may find yourself beginning to change your life for the better.
- You cannot beat the views you see when you are traveling in an RV.
- You don't need to buy too many things when you are in an RV. You are not held down by materialistic objects; your main focus is the experience and the joy it brings. Every moment in your life is one filled with what you encounter on your journey. If the journey is as important as the destination, then being attached to your belongings is no way to

experience that. However, in an RV, you are not distracted by such possessions. You are free to truly live the journey.

- Don't like your neighbors? Move.
- Don't like your surroundings? Move.
- Simply want to move? Move.
- Ever wanted to work and travel? Well, now is your chance.
- If you would like, you can stay in one place for a long time, get to know the people around you, take part in the community, and live among the locals.
- You learn to be independent, develop important life skills, and even build confidence. The RV life can influence you in many positive ways, maybe even making you become a better person.

HOW CAN YOU DO LAUNDRY?

- You can find campgrounds or parks where there are laundromats. By using the apps I recommended earlier, you can seek more information about various sites to find if they have laundry facilities.
- Make use of the local towns or nearby cities, if you can access them.
- In many cases, people learn to do their own laundry by hand. There are many occasions where you'll have to stay somewhere overnight, which means you can wash your clothes and leave them out to dry. However, make sure you are in a safe area before doing so in case you wake up the next morning and find your favorite polo shirt missing.
- Some RVs come with washers and dryers. You can also add them to your RV, but be very mindful of the space.

DO YOU FEEL SAFE ON THE ROAD?

- Typically, RVing is safe if you follow the rules and use a bit of common sense.
- Do not open the door in the middle of the night to people you do not recognize.
- Don't park your rig in neighborhoods littered with beer bottles and tagged with gang graffiti. That graffiti is not someone's idea of abstract expression—they are warnings.
- Don't keep your RV unlocked while you are outside. Don't keep your RV unlocked while you are inside, as well.
- Your RV probably comes with a bathroom. If you are in an unknown area, avoid public bathrooms.
- Stick to campgrounds and parks meant for RVs.
- I know it sounds nice to put up a sign outside saying, "Our home on wheels—Andy and his golden retriever, Fifi," but you are literally letting everyone know who is inside the RV. So the next time someone knocks on your door and calls your name, it may not be because they know you, but because they saw your cute sign with puppy stickers.
- Do not leave documents lying about. Keep them out of sight in a safe place.
- Crime on the road? It happens whether you are in an RV or not. If you were driving a vehicle and you felt something wrong while going down a particular path, you would immediately choose another way. Use the same sense when you are in an RV.
- I've mentioned this before, and it is worth mentioning again, keep your friends and family updated about you.

ISN'T GAS MILEAGE TERRIBLE?

- This depends on how you drive your RV. I recommended earlier that you should drive your RV slowly. This is not only for safety, but for gas consumption as well.
- Another important thing to note is that you should turn off the electronics or appliances not in use. There are RVers who leave their television on throughout their ride and then wonder where all the gas went the next morning. Make sure you are switching off the lights, appliances, or anything else using your RV's power.

WHEN WILL YOU START LIVING A NORMAL LIFE AGAIN?

There is no specific time period for you to get adjusted to the RV life. What is important is to focus on getting used to your new home and establish a routine for the various chores and activities you might take on while traveling on the road.

Additionally, make sure you enjoy the experience. Don't think of the whole process as one big chore or requirement. Appreciate the journey and everything else that comes with it.

CAN YOU RV FULL-TIME IN THE WINTER?

You can. Make sure you are aware of the local weather conditions so you prepare yourself for anything by getting the right gear.

Your RV itself can keep you warm from the elements, but the one thing you might have to be concerned about is the pile-up of snow outside. Make sure you have a shovel if you are traveling to places where the snow can accumulate.

HOW DO YOU STAY IN SHAPE WHILE ON THE ROAD?

The best part about being in an RV is the opportunity it brings to step outside and indulge in some outdoor activities, so don't hesitate to take a walk or go out hiking whenever you feel like it.

DO YOU GET TIRED OF LIVING IN A SMALL SPACE?

Some people do experience a sense of tiredness when it comes to living in an RV, but they more than make up for it by getting outdoors, being part of communities, or taking part in various activities. Just because you are in an RV does not mean you cannot head out and do something fun!

WHAT DO YOU DO WITH ALL THE POOP?

As mentioned before, you dump everything into special sewer holes or dump stations. I have even provided you tips on how to keep the black tank (or the poop tank) clean.

CONCLUSION

RVing is an adventure. It is about the journey and the way it changes your life. But getting started on this journey can be challenging, which is why you have this book.

We have discussed how you can get started with your RV adventure. We've talked about how you can downsize your home and then pack all the essential items into your RV. We've focused on the different types of RVs you can find and what you should look for when purchasing one. Then, we looked at how you can transition to your RV life, as well as how you can travel with your kids or pets. We have gone through the waste management process and how you can perform maintenance on your RV. We looked at camping and boondocking and even found ways for you to make money while you are on the road. Solo RV was also given a special focus in the book.

With all of this information, you can get started on your RV journey with confidence. Remember to take your time with a particular step if you are feeling unsure or lost. For example, if the downsizing process is turning out to be quite a challenge, then make sure you are not stressing about it or in a hurry. Take your time and do it right. This way, you'll find yourself facing less stress in the future. Additionally, get to know your RV. Familiarize yourself with all its features and mechanisms. Take it out for a test run before you head out on your RV adventure; be comfortable with your rig and the space within. Take your time to learn about the various RV communities, which will allow you to plan your journey better. You know how to store things, what you should do if are in need of assistance, what campgrounds you should go to, and more.

But most importantly, remember to enjoy your journey.

Happy RVing.

REFERENCES

Power, R. (2018). Consumers are Rejecting Materialism and Embracing Experiences — Here's How to Capitalize. Retrieved 14 September 2019, from https://www.inc.com/rhett-power/consumers-are-rejecting-materialism-embracing-experiences-heres-how-to-capitalize.html

RV Passive Income Guide, https://www.amazon.com/dp/B07XFT3NP5/

CPSIA information can be obtained
at www.ICGtesting.com
Printed in the USA
LVHW012235210820
663785LV00005B/194